UKULELE BEGINNERS JUMPSTART

Learn Basic Chords, Rhythms and Play Your First Songs

ANDY SCHNEIDER

HEAR THIS BOOK!

DOWNLOAD YOUR **FREE** AUDIO EXAMPLES OF THESE EXERCISES AT:

SEEINGMUSICBOOKS.com

SEEING MUSIC
METHOD BOOKS

© 2020 ANDY SCHNEIDER
WWW.SEEINGMUSICBOOKS.COM

Introduction

I love learning. I love getting new skills that give me new abilities. And, I love passing on those skills to others so that they can enjoy their own talents and new abilities. This book is for the absolute beginner. Welcome.

It's always a good time to start learning music and the ukulele. Students of any age can see real results from a good practice routine. Many, many adults and children have benefitted from my teaching method and I hope you'll soon have new abilities to make your own music.

In my years teaching guitar and stringed instruments and talking with other professional string players, I've noticed that we all have developed an ability to "see" the music we play on the fretboard of the instrument. We see the music we play as a simple relationship of shapes and relative positions. Look at these two shapes:

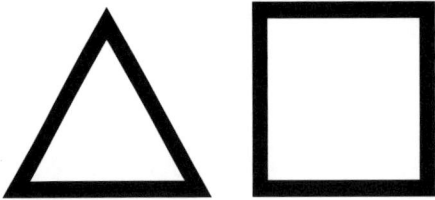

Just as you recognize the shapes above, stringed instrumentalists see music on the fretboard of their instrument. This is an inherently special gift we who play stringed instruments have been given. No other kind of instrument makes it so easy for the musician to have a visual roadmap of the music, making things like improvisation or transposing a song to another key so easy. Our fingers follow these maps to get to the music. This book will show you how to see music as simple shapes and use these shapes to more quickly and proficiently play and create music.

We'll be covering how music is constructed and 'looks' on the neck of the ukulele. While we won't get into any particular musical style or specific techniques, the information here is common to all Western music: Rock, Folk, Country, Pop, Classical, Jazz. While the first steps of ukulele playing are the same for everyone, the next few steps of learning chords can be taught many different ways. I'm going to walk you through what I believe is the fastest and most powerful way. Learning uke chords with a visual method makes it so much easier and minimizes memorization. You will develop life-long skills that you will use every day you pick up a ukulele.

Turn the page: you're about to "see" music!

SEEING MUSIC
METHOD BOOKS

CONTENTS

SELECTING YOUR FIRST UKULELE — 7

UKULELE CARE AND MAINTENANCE — 9

DAY 1 - PROPER PLAYING POSITION — 11

FRETBOARD DIAGRAMS — 13
- *A NOTE ABOUT FRETBOARD DIAGRAMS* — 15

DAY 2 - PLAYING SINGLE NOTES — 17
- *GOOD FRETTING TECHNIQUE* — 18
- *PUTTING IT ALL TOGETHER* — 19
- *ABOUT STAFF NOTATION* — 20

DAY 3 - THE C MAJOR SCALE — 23
- *THE AWESOME POWER OF SCALES* — 23
- *HOW TO PLAY THIS SCALE* — 24
- *MORE ABOUT MAJOR SCALES* — 24
- *ANOTHER WAY TO PLAY C MAJOR* — 25

DAY 4 - PLAYING YOUR FIRST CHORDS — 27
- *HOW TO PLAY CHORDS* — 27

KNOW YOUR UKULELE — 31

DAY 5 - PLAYING BARRE CHORDS — 33
WHAT ARE BARRE CHORDS? — 33
C MAJOR BARRE CHORD — 34
D MAJOR BARRE CHORDS — 36

DAY 6 - SCALES AND CHORDS — 39
HOW TO PLAY A D MAJOR SCALE — 39
ALL ABOUT SHARPS AND FLATS — 40

LEARNING YOUR FRETBOARD — 45
THE FIRST 5 FRETS — 45

DAY 7 - THE WALTZ — 47
3/4 TIME SIGNATURE — 47

DAY 8 - NEW STRUMMING PATTERNS — 49
WHAT GOES DOWN MUST COME UP — 49
HOW TO ADD UPSTROKES — 50

DAY 9 - MORE BARRE CHORDS — 53
LET'S GET MOVING! — 53

DAY 10 - MINOR CHORDS — 57
CHANGE MAJOR TO MINOR — 57
MORE MAGIC MINOR — 58
PUTTING CHORD FLAVORS TOGETHER — 60

DAY 11 - ALL ABOUT 7TH CHORDS — 63
EXTENDED CHORDS ADD COLOR — 63
DOMINANT 7TH CHORDS — 64
MINOR 7TH CHORDS — 67
MAJOR 7TH CHORDS — 68

DAY 12 - PLAY YOUR FIRST SONGS — 71
HOW TO PLAY JINGLE BELLS — 71
HOW TO PLAY HAPPY BIRTHDAY — 72
HOW TO PLAY A BLUES SONG — 73
HOW TO PLAY A ROCK AND ROLL SONG — 73
ROCK AND ROLL WITH MINOR CHORDS — 74

MILESTONES IN MUSIC — 77

CHORD AND NOTE REFERENCE — 79

UKULELE BEGINNERS JUMPSTART

SELECTING YOUR FIRST UKULELE

There are many choices to be made when picking a new uke. Not only are there different looks, but there are different sizes and designs that affect tone and playability. No one instrument works for all musicians. It's also tricky to know what you'll prefer in a few months or years as you develop as a musician. Let's look at some of the biggest factors ukulele buyers face so you can find a great one to play for many years to come.

Size and Playability

This bit is crucial. Ukuleles come in many sizes, often described by their scale length. *Scale* is literally the length of the string, measured from the bridge to the nut (see chapter *Know Your Ukulele* for details). If you're a tall person, you may want to look for a baritone or even a bass ukulele. Most ukuleles are called *concert* or *tenor*, which refer to the scale lengths. Tenor is slightly longer. Baritone and bass ukuleles use a tuning different from that described in this book.

Another factor is the playability or *action* of the neck. Action refers to how easily the ukulele plays. For good action, the strings must be fairly close to the frets, but not so close they create a buzzing sound. If you're unfamiliar with how good action feels, ask someone with experience for their opinion of your ukulele candidate. Since the action of most ukes can be adjusted by a technician, if you already own one, you may be able to improve its playability at your local repair shop.

From time-to-time, such as if the instrument is dropped or just over a great deal of time, the action changes and the uke will need a little adjustment. This operation is usually refered to as a *set-up* and involves adjusting the height of the strings, the bow of the neck (yes, necks are supposed to be slightly bowed) and sometimes adjusting the string slots in the nut.

Price

This is a big one, obviously. Some people like to be value-minded and find an inexpensive uke to begin their study. There is nothing wrong with that. Some people like to make a big investment right away, buying a beautiful ukulele from a well-reputed manufacturer. Perhaps it helps them stay motivated to learn or they view it as an investment. Either way, there are great instruments for beginners at all prices. Generally, more expensive ukes have a better tone and some high-quality features, such as more adjustability for the owner's playing style.

Strings

Most any uke will have nylon strings. Not being made from metal, nylon strings have a much lower tension than metal strings. Metal strings should never be used on a ukulele. The higher tension of metal strings can actually damage the instrument. There are such things as aluminum wrapped nylon strings which are meant for very low pitched strings, such as on tenor, baritone or bass ukes. But in general, avoid using anything except nylon strings meant for a ukulele.

Quality of Tuners

This is a bigger issue than you might think. Good quality tuners turn very smoothly and help keep the ukulele in tune. Poor ones make it difficult to tune or even cause the uke to slip out of tune. If you can, try their feel. If you're buying without being able to try them, know that the cost of the instrument is generally an indicator of the quality. Not always, but generally more expensive ukes come with more high-quality tuners.

Pickups

Most ukuleles don't have pickups but these days, more are hitting the market with internal pickups. These generally use a pickup located inside the bridge, out of sight. If you plan to perform in public, it's really handy to have an internal pickup. The venue soundperson will thank you. If you will be recording in the studio, microphones are generally used instead of the internal pickup. Either way, having a pickup or not having one shouldn't affect your enjoyment of your uke.

Other Fancy Stuff

There's lots of things that get added to ukes to either dress them up or add functionality. Adornments like inlays and binding add visual appeal but not playability. Examples of functional upgrades include pickups, on-board electronic tuners and equalizers (EQs).

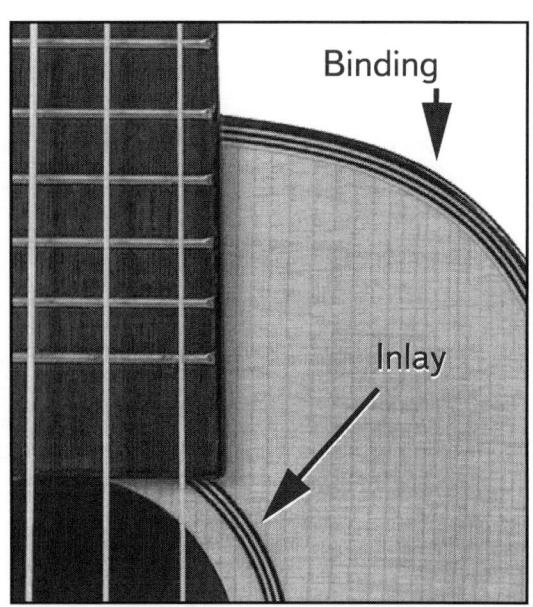

FIG.1 - INLAY AND BINDING

8 UKULELE BEGINNERS JUMPSTART: A SEEING MUSIC METHOD BOOK

UKULELE CARE AND MAINTENANCE

Storage

Ukes are a lot like people: They don't like things too hot or too cold, too wet or too dry. Avoid leaving your ukukeke in very hot or cold places, like a car. A great rule of thumb is, if you would be uncomfortable with the temperature or humidity of a place, don't leave your uke there.

When putting away your instrument, a hard-shell case is the safest location. A ukulele stand is also acceptable. Avoid leaning your uke against a wall or furniture. If it slips and falls over, it could easily be damaged or broken. Also, avoid leaving it near heaters, radiators or even in bright sunshine.

Cleaning

Keep your ukulele clean with guitar polish and a soft rag or polish cloth. Generally, a light spritz of polish and wiping with the polish cloth is all that's necessary. Your instrument's manufacturer may have special recommendations to follow.

Replacing Strings

Strings wear out over time and with use. If you see any discoloration or evidence of wear, like dents where the strings meet the frets, buy a new set of strings and have them replaced by a technician. If you're replacing strings yourself, be aware that they can spring up and poke your eyes. Consider wearing safety eyewear. Seriously. Your eyes deserve protection.

If you can see music, why not listen to a book?

HEAR THIS BOOK!

DOWNLOAD YOUR **FREE** AUDIO EXAMPLES OF THESE EXERCISES AT:

SEEINGMUSICBOOKS.com

DAY 1 - PROPER PLAYING POSITION

Lay a Great Foundation

Great music begins with correct posture and instrument position. You can choose to stand or sit. Hold the ukulele to your body, with the neck pointing parallel to the ground or just slightly upward. If the neck sags too low to the floor, you'll have to reach farther with your left hand and playing will be difficult and uncomfortable.

Your right forearm will wrap around the instrument body and hold it in place. You may find a strap helps hold the uke in place and prevents it from falling. Straps aren't essential, but feel free to try one.

FIG.2 - PROPER UKULELE POSITION

FIG.3 - GOOD HAND POSITION

Notice in the pictures how the fretting hand thumb is directly behind the neck and the wrist is straight. A straight wrist is essential for good technique, but also the hardest part for many students to achieve. In the next chapter, we'll see why.

While you're learning the fundamentals, the more time you spend focused on correct posture and technique, the faster you'll get where you want to go. In fact, refer to this chapter often. Remember to always check your alignment and return to good hand, instrument and body position if they slip.

The uke is tuned G, C, E and A. If you're experienced you can tune by ear against some other instrument like a piano, but the easiest way to tune is to buy an electronic tuner. Many are available inexpensively. Make sure you get a chromatic tuner, one that can tune any note. Some guitar tuners are specially made to respond to the exact frequencies of the guitar's strings which are different from a uke's.

More about tuning: Some ukuleles have a low G string but most have a high G. That is, the pitch of this 4th string is actually higher than that of the 3rd string C. It's unusual for stringed instruments not to have their strings progressively going from low pitch to high, but this is the traditional tuning of concert ukuleles.

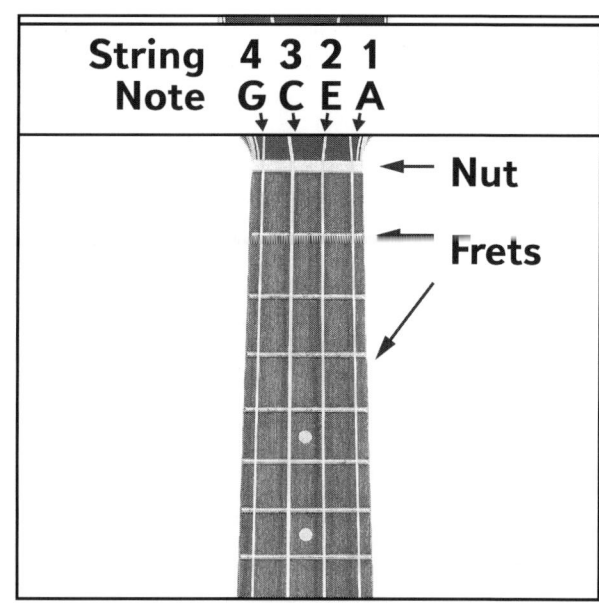

FIG.4 - STRING NAMES AND NUMBERS

Alternatively, there are lots of great tuners available for smartphones and tablets. Many of these apps are free, so if you have a smart device, check its app store.

The strings of the ukulele are numbered starting from the highest pitch string, the one closest to the floor when held in playing position. The highest and lightest string is the first string and the one furtherest from it is the fourth string.

A Note About Fingernails

Long fingernails and uke playing don't really go well together. If you've got long nails on your fretting hand, you'll find they get in the way of good finger position. They also tend to dig in the wood of the fretboard. Long nails on the picking hand tend to get scuffed or interfere with fingerstyle picking. While long nails may look pretty, you may have to make a tough choice to cut them.

Ready to get more from your fretboard?

Loads of great exercises to put your memory to work.

seeingmusicbooks.com

12 UKULELE BEGINNERS JUMPSTART: A SEEING MUSIC METHOD BOOK

FRETBOARD DIAGRAMS

How to Read Fretboard Diagrams

You're ready to start learning some notes. The diagrams in this book are kind of like pictures of what you'll see when you look at your ukulele.

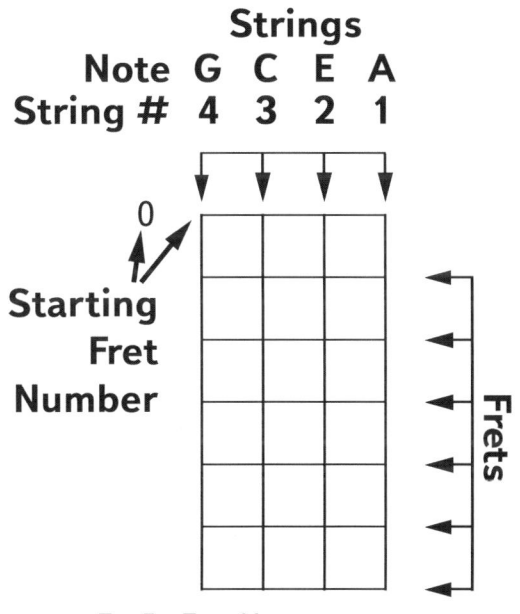

FIG.5 - FRET NOTATION

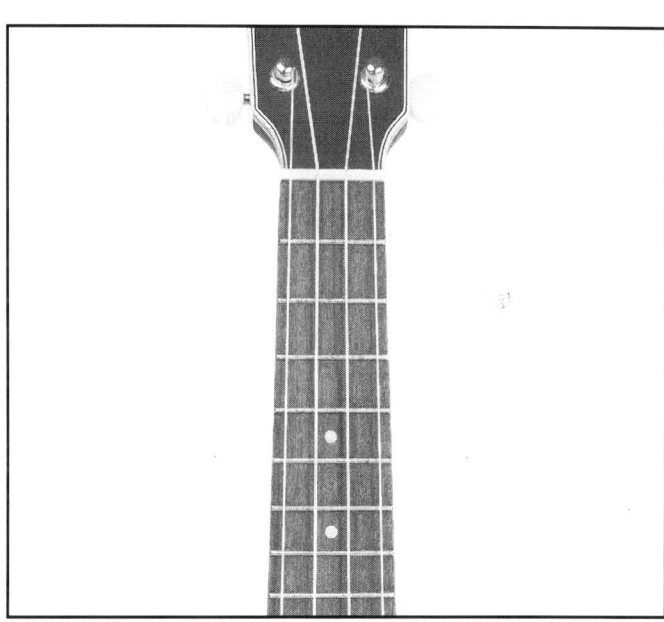

FIG.6 - FRETBOARD

Hold your ukulele upright in front of you and look at fretboard. The strings run up and down, the frets run horizontally. That is the view used in fretboard diagrams.

Let's try playing our first note. As indicated in Figure 7, play open G, the 4th string. An open circle indicates an open string, one that is played without fretting with the left hand.

With your picking hand, feel free to use a lightweight pick or your thumb or index finger. For now, do whatever is comfortable.

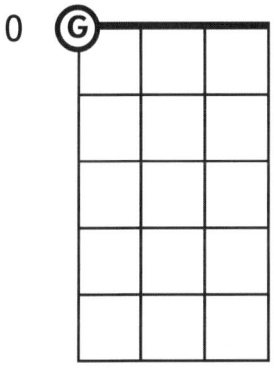

FIG.7 - OPEN 4TH STRING

FRETBOARD DIAGRAMS 13

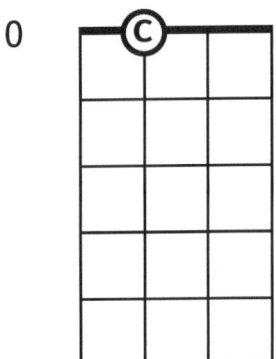

Did that go well? Try another, this time open C, the 3rd string.

FIG.8 - OPEN 3RD STRING

Figure 9 tells you to play the note found at the black dot on the 3rd string at the 3rd fret. It's the 3rd fret because it's three frets higher up the neck than the "0" in the upper-left corner of the diagram. The zero indicates that the diagram begins at the nut or "zeroth" fret.

The "2" next to the black dot indicates you'll use the 2nd finger of your fretting hand as in Figure 10.

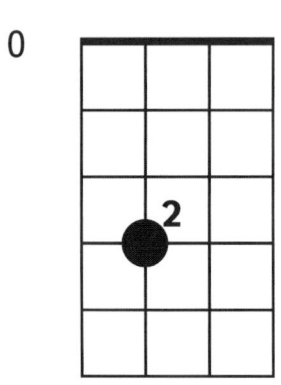
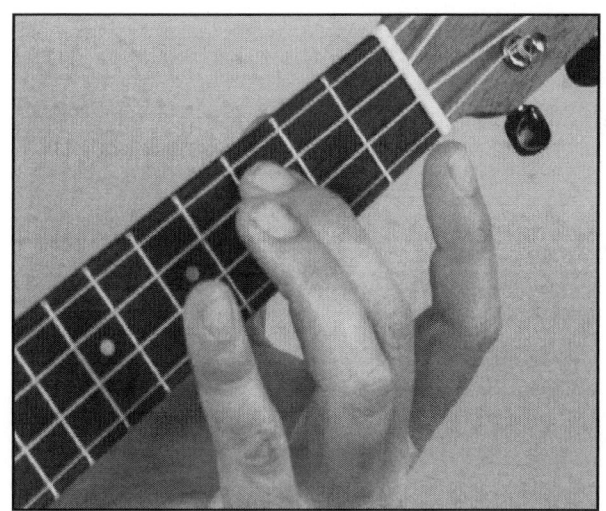

FIG.9 - FRET NOTATION   FIG.10 - LEFT-HAND FINGERING

On these diagrams, a filled in circle indicates that you'll put your finger at that fret. Actually, you'll put your finger just behind the fret, not right on top of the fret. The fret, not your finger, is what stops the vibration of the string and changes its length.

Keeping your finger pressed with medium pressure, just behind the fret will produce the clearest and best sound.

14 UKULELE BEGINNERS JUMPSTART: A SEEING MUSIC METHOD BOOK

Don't confuse a fretboard diagram with a musical staff. Music staves indicate pitch and rhythm. Fretboard diagrams like Figure 9 are like a roadmap, showing you where to place your fingers.

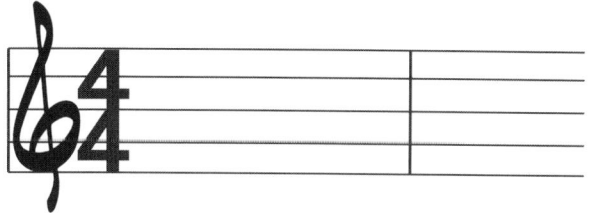

FIG.11 - MUSICAL STAFF

A NOTE ABOUT FRETBOARD DIAGRAMS

Most other books place the dot in-between the fret lines. This kind of diagram is helpful for getting quick answers about where fretting fingers belong, but this book also demonstrates the reason *why* notes are placed where they are. Understanding the "why" of music actually makes it easier to learn and memorize. You'll start to make associations about chords and scales that will amplify your learning.

So, when you see a dot in this book, you'll know that it is showing you the note to be played and that you'll place your finger just behind that fret to hear it.

SOUNDCHECK

Fretboard diagrams indicate where to find a note and what finger to use to play it.

The number in the upper-left corner of a fretboard diagram indicates on which fret the diagram begins.

Fretboard diagrams should not be confused with musical staves.

FRETBOARD DIAGRAMS 15

16 UKULELE BEGINNERS JUMPSTART: A SEEING MUSIC METHOD BOOK

DAY 2 - PLAYING SINGLE NOTES

MILESTONE

As you pass each milestone, take a moment to recall previous lessons.

Have a seat with your ukulele in good playing position.

Ready to start making music? Let's start with some open string notes.

You'll remember these notes from yesterday's lesson about the names of the strings.

Let's review: Start by playing open G. Using either your left-hand thumb or a pick, sound open G on the 4th string.

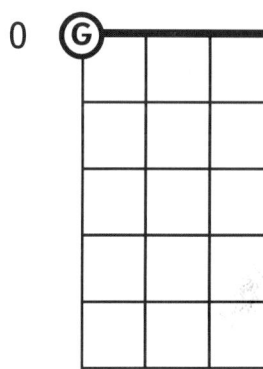

FIG.12 - OPEN 4TH STRING (G)

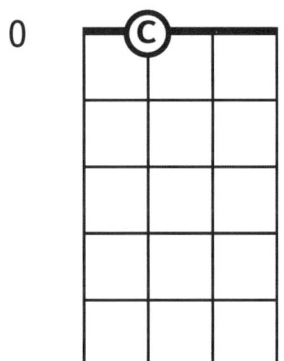

Now try open C. Feel free to look down at your left hand so you cleanly sound just the 3rd string. It's easy to hit other strings in the process, so keep focused on just hitting the C string.

FIG.13 - OPEN 3RD STRING (C)

PLAYING SINGLE NOTES 17

GOOD FRETTING TECHNIQUE

Here is the note D on the 3rd string. Give it a try, place your 2nd finger just behind the 2nd fret.

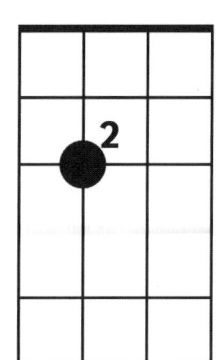

Fig.14 - 3rd String D

On the 4th string, the 2nd fret is A. Use the 2nd finger of your fretting hand on the 2nd fret, as well.

Now repeat, playing D on the 3rd string, then A on the 4th. Do this a few more times.

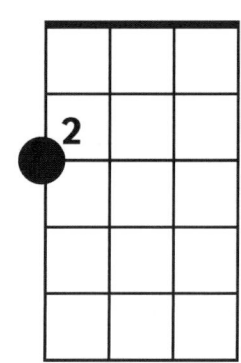

Fig.15 - 4th String A

SOUNDCHECK

Now, how do things sound? Are you getting any buzzes? Is the note full and ringing? Most students need several days of this exercise before the notes sound clean and pleasant. If you're having trouble, make certain that your fretting finger is very near the fret. This is crucial. In fact, you'll be so close that you're almost on top of the fret. When you get the feel of it, it will make everything else easier. Keep trying!

Also, keep your wrist straight, not bent. Remember that tilting the neck up and keeping the fretboard near your shoulder will make this easier. Playing ukulele should never be uncomfortable, so if your fingers, hands, arms or anywhere else starts to hurt, stop right away. Sometimes fingertips get sore after a practice session, especially if a player is just starting out. In time, callouses develop, making playing less uncomfortable.

18 UKULELE BEGINNERS JUMPSTART: A SEEING MUSIC METHOD BOOK

PUTTING IT ALL TOGETHER

Every note has a beginning and an end, right? While there's only one way to pick a string, there are two ways to stop it. Let's put it all together, starting and stopping each of the four notes.

Play open C, then open G. Start each note with your pick or thumb, then stop each note by lightly touching the strings with your right fingers. Try it again, picking the note, then "catching" the strings to stop the note.

Similarly, pick D then A. These are fretted notes, so if you let up the pressure with your fretting hand, the note will stop ringing. Give it a try. Tinker with the speed and pressure change with your fretting hand until the note stops cleanly.

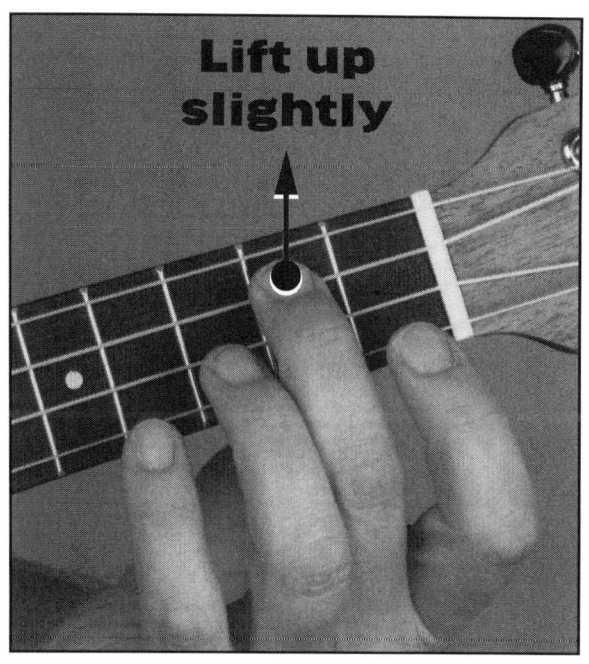

FIG.16 - LEFT-HAND MUTING

Ok, now let's stop these notes a different way. This time, you'll use your picking hand to stop the note. This is called palm muting and it's like putting the brakes on a car. You'll use the bottom of your picking hand, the soft bottom edge of your hand that's between your pinky and wrist. Pick a note, then use your palm's edge to stop it. Is the note stopping cleanly? See how fast you can go from picking the note to stopping it. See how slowly you can do the same. Pretty neat, huh?

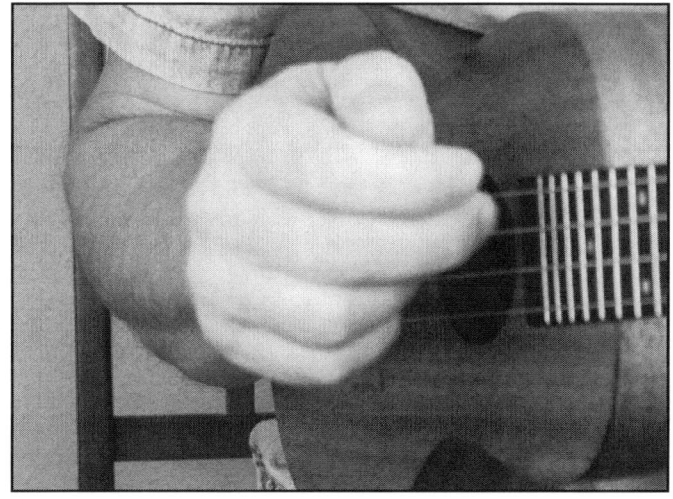

FIG.17 - PICKING POSITION

FIG.18 - PALM MUTING

PLAYING SINGLE NOTES 19

ABOUT STAFF NOTATION

Music staffs are a great, efficient way to describe rhythm. Here is a staff indicating Treble Clef and time signature. Treble Clef means it's describing upper notes (not bass notes) and the time signature tells us how to count. Most, but not all, music is in 4, meaning we count one measure "1, 2, 3, 4." The top number 4 is that number. The bottom number means that what we are counting is quarter notes. Just as with apples or dollars, a quarter is 1/2 of a half. A half is 1/2 of a whole.

FIG.19 - 4/4 TIME SIGNATURE

So, our staff here indicates we are in the Treble Clef. The song is in 4/4 time, which means there are 4 beats of quarter notes in each measure. A measure is indicated by the vertical lines on the staff.

Figure 20 shows a quarter-note rest. Where notes (or in this book, hash marks) tell us when to play, rests tell us when not to play. Take a little rest!

FIG.20 - QUARTER-NOTE REST

Today's Assignment

Let's practice starting and stopping notes cleanly. The hash marks on the staff tell you when to play a note, the name of the note is above it. The rests tell you when to mute the strings for silence.

Rhythm Tip: Slowly say "One, Two, Three, Four". Now, say the same thing, but whisper on "Two" and "Four". It should sound like "ONE, two, THREE, four". Now, imitate that with your uke, "ONE, two, THREE, four". Keep repeating this exercise, slowly at first.

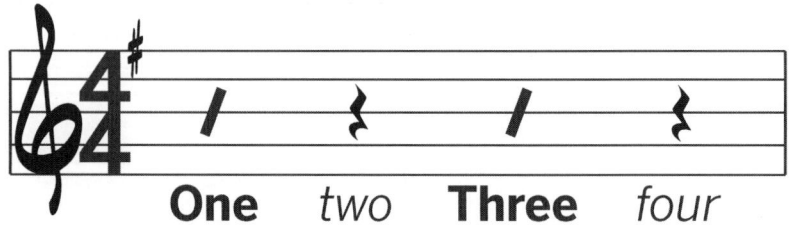

FIG.21 - COUNTING QUARTER-NOTES AND RESTS

20 UKULELE BEGINNERS JUMPSTART: A SEEING MUSIC METHOD BOOK

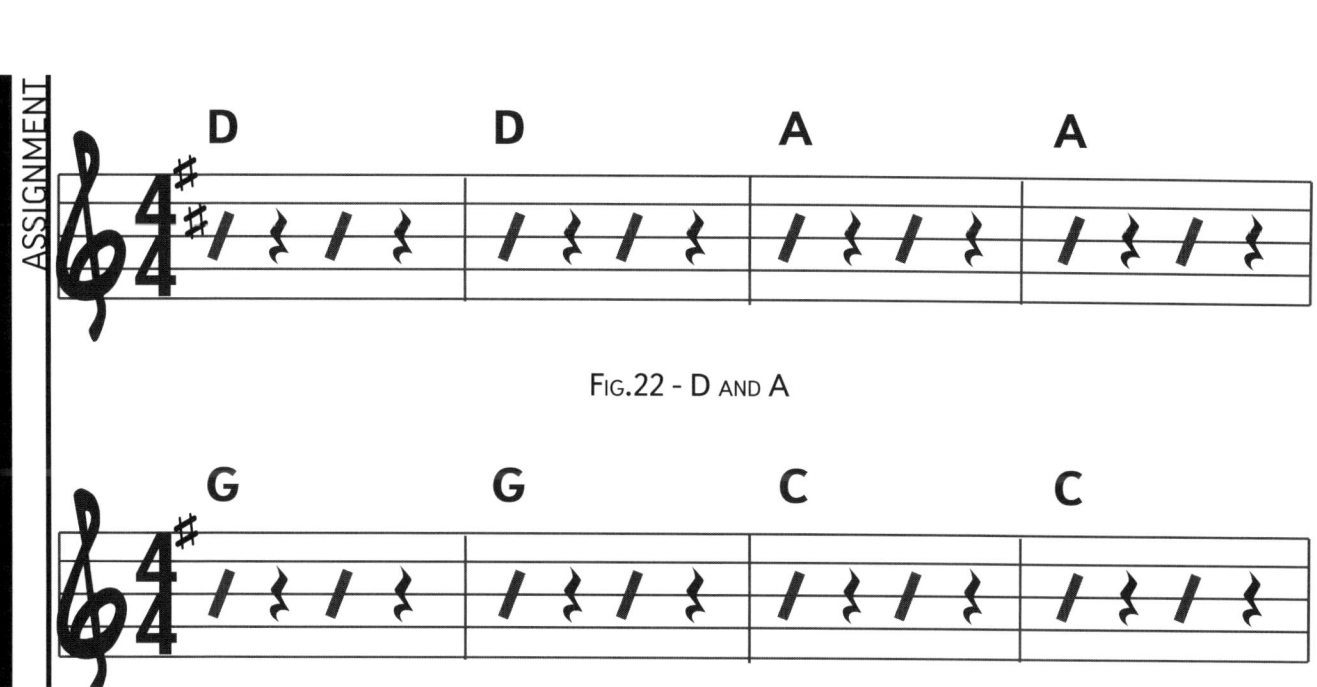

Fig.22 - D and A

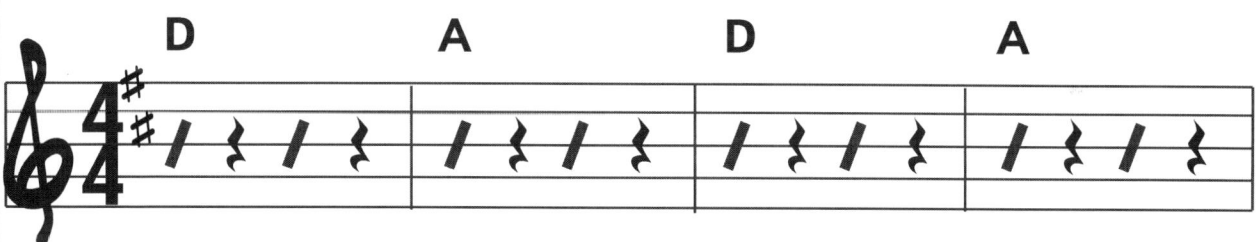

Fig.23 - G and C

Fig.24 - D and A Alternating

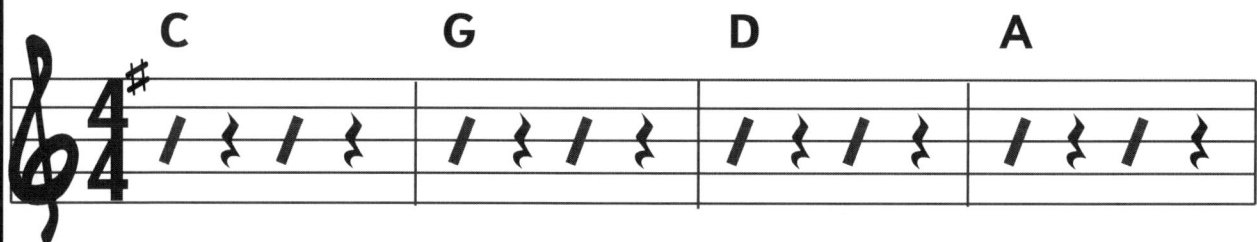

Fig.25 - G and C Alternating

Fig.26 - C, G, D and A

PLAYING SINGLE NOTES 21

You've got big ideas. Keep them organized.

SEEING MUSIC METHOD BOOKS

Over 100 Pages of Clean Single-Staff Paper
Clean Design and Easy-to-Use Matte Finish
Saves Time and Clutter in Your Music Space
Includes a Fill-In Table of Contents to Keep Track of Your Compositions

Lots of Clean Single-Staff Sheets to Organize Your Music

JUST BLANK STAFF PAPER

ANDY SCHNEIDER

ALL LEVELS

DAY 3 - THE C MAJOR SCALE

MILESTONE

At the 2nd fret, play D on the 3rd string and A on the 4th string.

Remember: Your fretting finger should be just behind the fret; the closer, the better.

THE AWESOME POWER OF SCALES

Scales are awesome because ALL music comes from them! Melodies come from scales. Chords come from scales. And scales are easy to memorize, which will make learning chords easy, too.

Take a look at the C Major scale. The notes of the C Major scale in order are C, D, E, F, G, A, B and C.

FIG.27 - C MAJOR SCALE NOTE NAMES

All the notes here are separated by a whole-step, except those indicated by the "^" symbol. Those are separated by a half-step. On the ukulele, two notes that are one fret apart are separated by a half-step. Two half-steps equals one whole step, which would be two frets distance.

Again, most notes here are one whole-step apart, with the exception being those separated by a half-step.

THE C MAJOR SCALE 23

HOW TO PLAY THIS SCALE

In Figure 28, start on the open 3rd string. It's indicated by the circle with the "X" through it. This is the root, C.

Play the C, then add your 2nd finger just behind the 2nd fret on the same string. Play this note, D.

Now, you can release these notes. Play the open 2nd string. This is E. Adding your 1st finger to the 1st fret on this string, play F. With each new note, do you hear the pitches getting higher?

Keeping your finger on F, add your 3rd finger to the 3rd fret of the 2nd string. This is G. Now you can release that string and move on to the open 1st string, A. Now add your 2nd finger to the 2nd fret and play B. Keeping that finger in place, add your 3rd finger to the 3rd fret and play the high C.

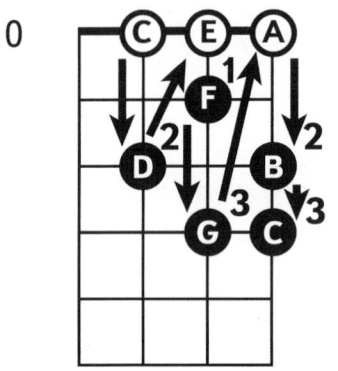

Repeat this scale a few times. The pitch you hear with each successive note should be higher than the last.

Figure 29 is the same scale with a different notation. The X's through two dots indicate a very important note: The root of the scale. In this particular scale, that note is C and so the scale is called C Major.

Whenever playing a scale, keep the root firmly in mind.

FIG.28 - C MAJOR SCALE

MORE ABOUT MAJOR SCALES

A major scale is a series of whole and half-steps.

A half-step is the distance between two notes that are one fret apart. A whole-step is equal to two half-steps.

In all major scales, the half-steps are between the 3rd and 4th notes (or *degrees*) and the 7th and root degrees. All the other notes are a whole step apart, or the equivalent of two frets in distance from each other.

In the C Major scale, the half-steps are between E and F and between B and C. Take note of them in Figure 28.

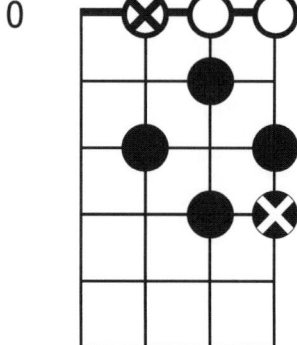

FIG.29 - C MAJOR SCALE

24 UKULELE BEGINNERS JUMPSTART: A SEEING MUSIC METHOD BOOK

ANOTHER WAY TO PLAY C MAJOR

Ukulele is a great instrument because it offers a couple of different ways to play the same notes. Here is another way to play the same C Major scale. These scales are great for learning the notes on the fingerboard.

Again, start on the open 3rd string, C. This time, add your 1st finger at the 2nd fret of that string. This is D.

Keeping it there, add your 3rd finger to the 5th fret and play E. Again keeping your finger there, add your 4th finger, your pinky, to the next fret, fret 5. This is F.

Remember, these are the same notes you played before, but some are just found in new locations on the fretboard.

Now for the big surprise! The next note to play is the open 4th string, G. Pick it now. Hear how the pitch got higher? This is the somewhat unusual thing about the ukulele. On most stringed instruments, the higher numbered strings are always lower in pitch. On the ukulele, the 4th string is actually *higher* than the 3rd. It's an irregularity that makes ukulele a wonderful and unique instrument.

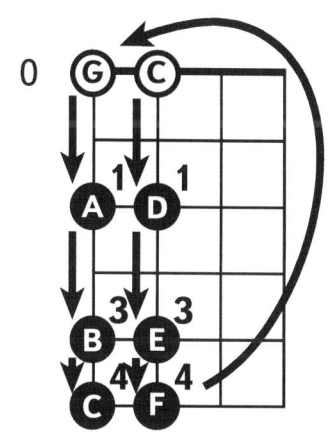

FIG.30 - C MAJOR SCALE

Complete the scale by playing the open 4th string G, then playing each note successively as in Figure 31. You will end again with on high C using your 4th finger.

Repeat this scale a few times. Do you see how the note order and fingering are the same on both the 3rd and 4th strings?

MEMORY SUPERPOWER

To easily remember the fingering of the C Major scale, use this tip:

On the C-string, you use fingers 1, 3 and 4. Then on the G-string, you also use fingers 1, 3 and 4.

When you say it to yourself a few times, it even starts to sound kind of musical. Say, "Open, 1 3 4, Open 1 3 4."

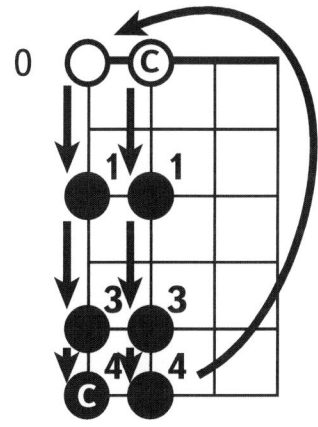

FIG.31 - C MAJOR SCALE

THE C MAJOR SCALE 25

Today's Assignment

Sure, scales help your fingers get used to finding their way around the neck, but aren't they a little boring? No! They will be your superpower, soon letting you access any chord, any melody, anytime.

Play C Major starting with the lowest note (C on the 3rd string) and ending with the highest note (C on the 1st string). Play this a few times until you can make the string changes easily and smoothly.

If you find it difficult to reach all the notes, stop and examine your wrist. Is it bent? It shouldn't be. When your wrist is straight, you'll have the greatest reach possible. Make some adjustments to the angle of your instrument, your wrist, arm and possibly even your uke height. Review the chapter "Proper Playing Position".

After you successfully can play all 8 notes going up the scale, play them in reverse order, descending down the scale. Start with the top note, C on the 1st string, and work your way down to C on the 3rd string.

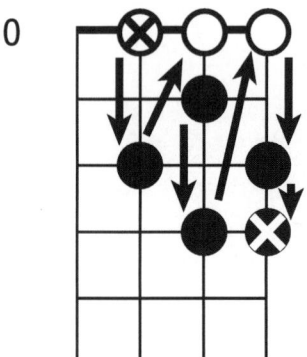

Fig.32 - C Major Ascending

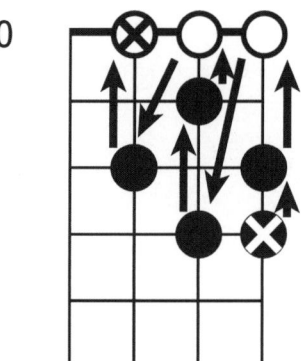

Fig.33 - C Major Descending

26 UKULELE BEGINNERS JUMPSTART: A SEEING MUSIC METHOD BOOK

DAY 4 - PLAYING YOUR FIRST CHORDS

MILESTONE

Play the C Major scale in the second pattern you learned yesterday. It is the scale on just the 3rd and 4th strings.

Now, play it again but stop on the 5th note, G. It is the note on the open 4th string.

Take note! That D is in both of the chords you're about to learn.

HOW TO PLAY CHORDS

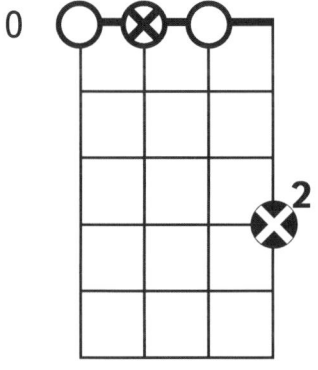

FIG.34 - C MAJOR CHORD

Examine the fretboard diagram at left. The numbers indicate which finger to use. Remember, open circles are open strings.

On the 1st string at the 3rd fret, place your 2nd finger.

Now give a little strum to all four strings together with a downward motion as though they were one big note.

This is a C Major chord and is really fun to play because fretting it only takes one finger!

FIG.35 - C MAJOR HAND POSITION

FIG.36 - C MAJOR PLAYER'S VIEW

PLAYING YOUR FIRST CHORDS

Now, try this G Major chord. G Major and C Major are two chords that are found in lots of songs.

Start by fingering the notes one at a time. On the 3rd string, place your 1st finger on the 2nd fret. Now lay that finger down across the 2nd and 1st strings as well. Your 1st finger is barring all three strings at the 2nd fret.

Now on the 2nd string, add your 2nd finger. It will be on the 3rd fret. Don't let it touch the adjacent strings, just the 2nd string.

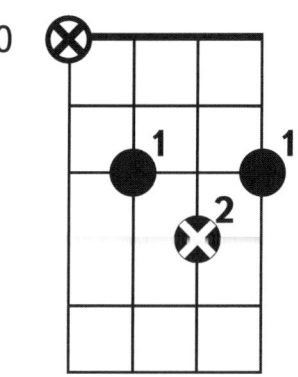

FIG.37 - G MAJOR CHORD

Give a gentle strum across all 4 strings. Slow your strum down to hear each note individually. All four notes should ring well. Adjust your fret fingers if necessary. Usually, it takes a little tinkering to get a feel for how much pressure is needed, and just how close to the fret the fingertips should be.

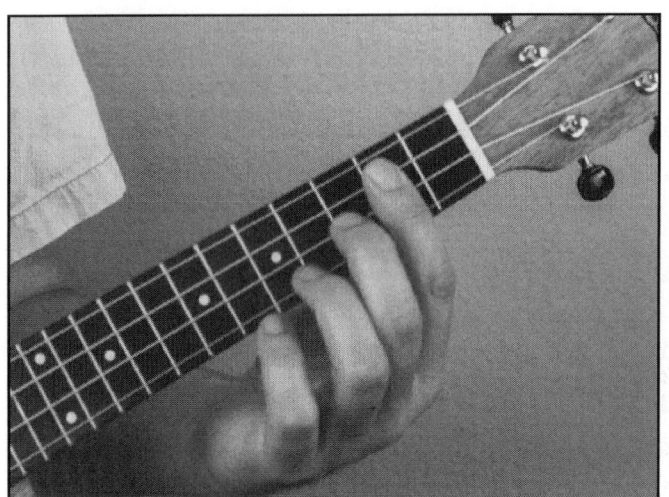

FIG.38 - G MAJOR HAND POSITION

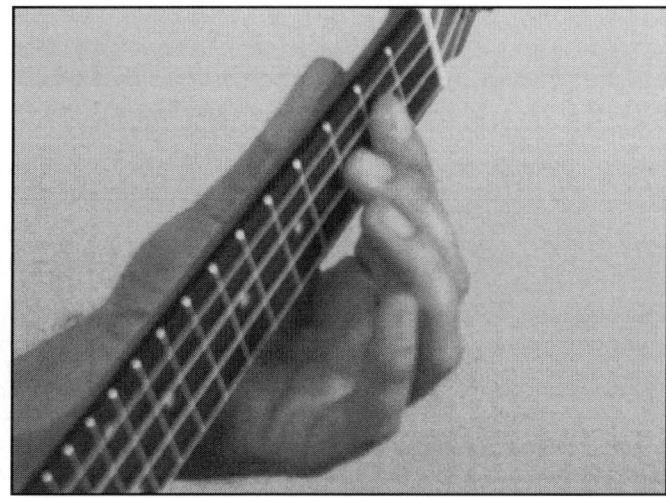

FIG.39 - G MAJOR PLAYER'S VIEW

You did it! You just learned your first two complete chords! This is no small feat and your fingers and brain probably feel a little like spaghetti about now. Every string player feels that way when they learn their first chords. Give yourself a big ol' pat on the back!

The great news is that it gets easier every time you do it.

SOUNDCHECK

You've already seen quarter-notes. Here is a combination rhythm that uses both quarter-notes and half-notes. A half-note takes the same amount of time as 2 quarter-notes. Out loud, count, "One, Two, Three, Four". Each word is a quarter-note. A half-note would be held for a two-count, like "One, Two" or "Three, Four".

Play these with the chords from Figures 34 and 37.

FIG. 40 - G C RHYTHM 1

Here's a variation, with the half-note on the first two beats of each measure.

FIG. 41 - G C RHYTHM 2

You know, this is starting to sound a lot like music! Congratulate yourself, musician!

Today's Assignment

Try these mini-songs using whole chords, G Major and C Major (Figs 34 and 37). Use a downward motion for each strum.

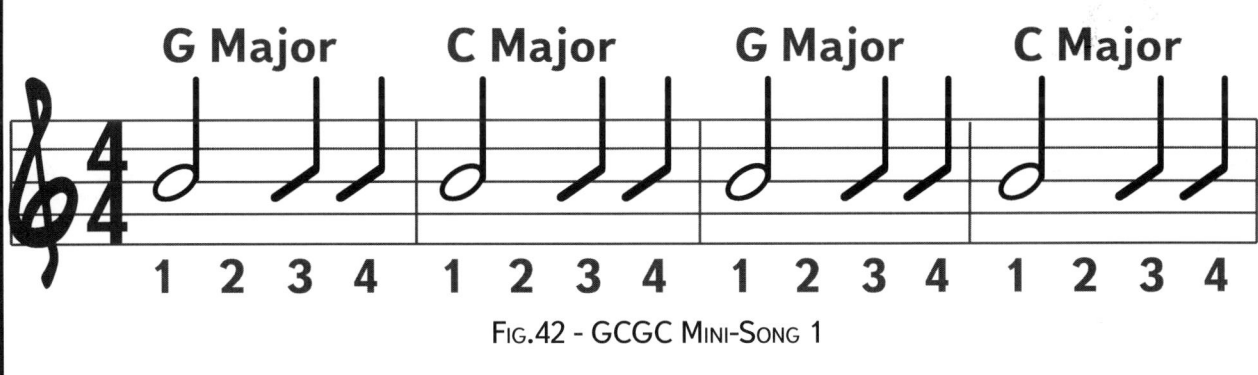

FIG. 42 - GCGC MINI-SONG 1

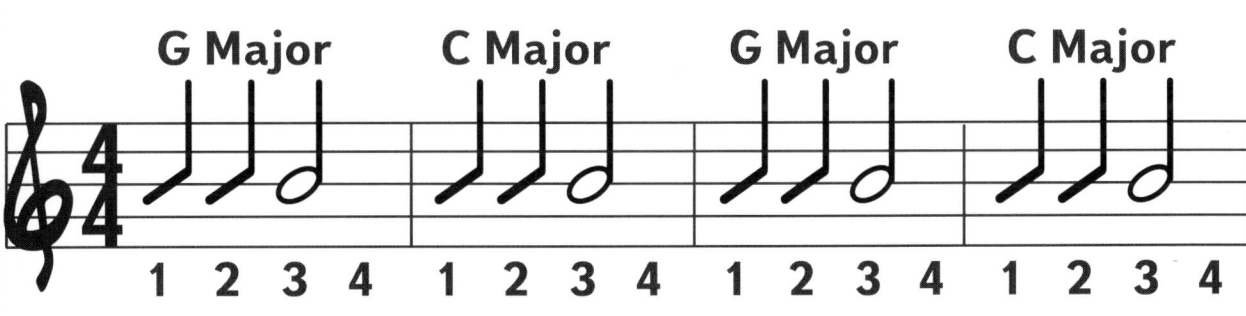

FIG. 43 - GCGC MINI-SONG 2

KNOW YOUR UKULELE

Ukulele

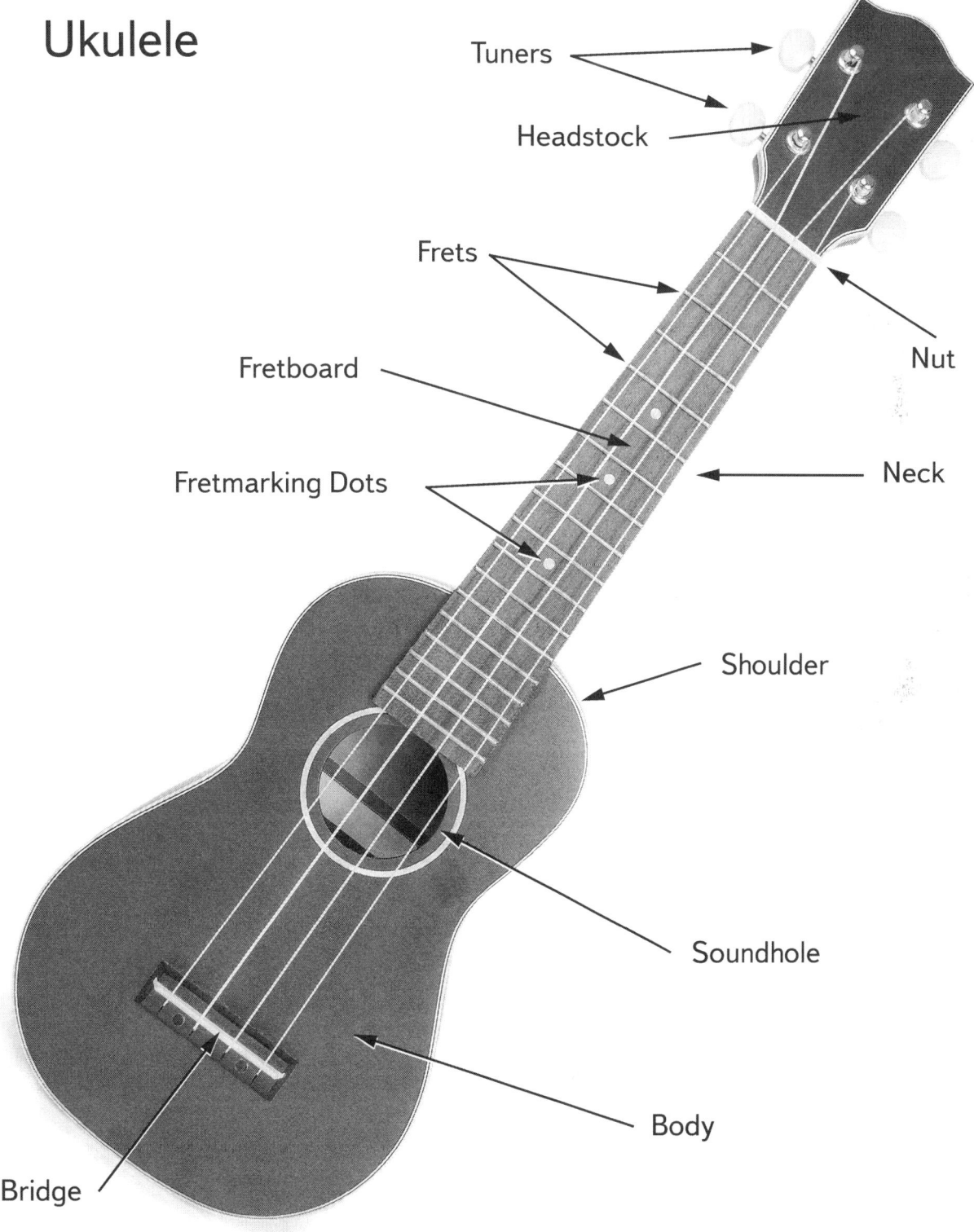

Fig.44 - Ukulele

32 UKULELE BEGINNERS JUMPSTART: A SEEING MUSIC METHOD BOOK

DAY 5 - PLAYING BARRE CHORDS

MILESTONE

Play the C Major and G Major chords from yesterday.

Those are open-string versions of those chords. They rely on open-strings. There are also versions of those chords which use no open-strings and they will come in very handy.

WHAT ARE BARRE CHORDS?

A barre chord is a chord where one of your fingers plays more than one string. In general, they don't rely on open strings and so can be moved up and down the fingerboard to create new chords. Rather than play with just the fingertip, players lay the finger across several strings at once, so different strings are contacting the finger in several place.

Examine the fretboard diagrams below. At left, the open-string version of the G Major chord you've learned. At right, the barre chord version. Notice that while they share many notes, the barre chord version doesn't use the open 4th string. It also has a bit different fingering which will come in handy, as you will see later.

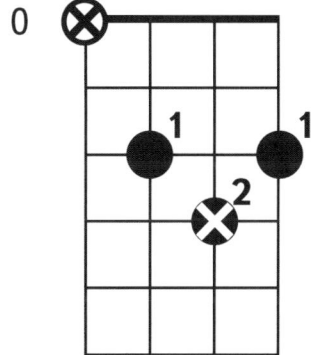

FIG.45 - G MAJOR CHORD WITH OPEN STRINGS

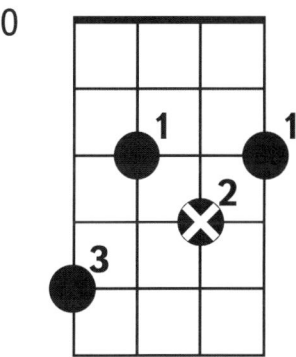

FIG.46 - G MAJOR BARRE CHORD

Start by placing the tip of your 1st finger on the 3rd string at the 2nd fret. Play that note. Now, roll that finger down so it's laying across the next few strings. Just like a log laying across train tracks, you'll use your 1st finger to play two notes. With your 1st finger barring those notes, try playing the note on string 3 and then string 1. Do they both sound good and sustain well?

FIG.47 - G MAJOR BARRE HAND POSITION

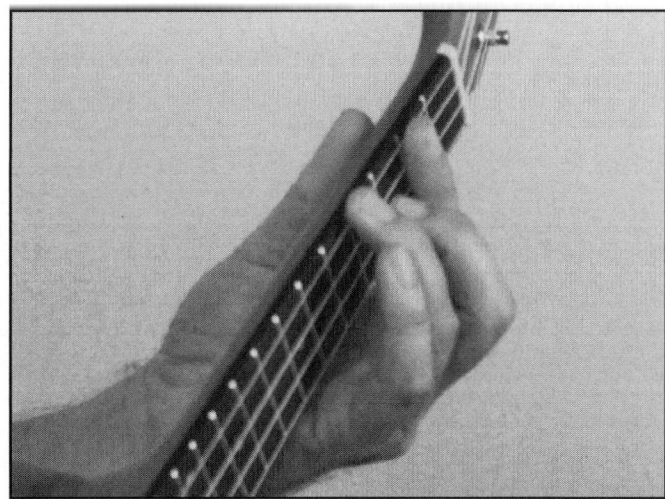

FIG.48 - G MAJOR BARRE PLAYER'S VIEW

Now add your 2nd finger to the 2nd string at the 3rd fret. Give a strum to all three, notes, then play each note individually to be sure your fretting hand is positioned well.

Keeping those fingers in place, reach your 3rd finger across the neck and place it at the 4th string, 4th fret. Now play all 4 strings of the barre chord. Did it work? You may need to give a little arch to your 3rd finger so it clears the first three strings without touching them.

At first, using your finger as a barre may feel awkward. Keep trying it. Your brain will keep tuning the exact position of your fingers until this becomes much easier and sounds great, too.

C MAJOR BARRE CHORD

Begin playing this chord with your 1st finger on the 2nd string at the 3rd fret. Play that note, just to make sure you're in good position near the fret.

Now, let that finger lay down so it plays the 1st string at the 2nd fret, as well. Your 1st finger is now barring these two notes.

Next, place the tip of your 2nd finger on the 3rd string at the 4th fret. Play that note. Keeping those fingers there, add your 3rd finger to the 4th string, 5th fret.

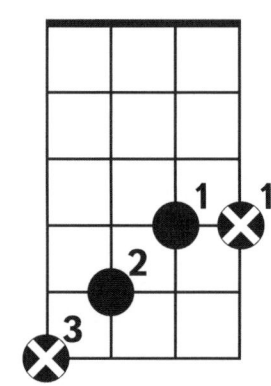

FIG.49 - C MAJOR BARRE

34 UKULELE BEGINNERS JUMPSTART: A SEEING MUSIC METHOD BOOK

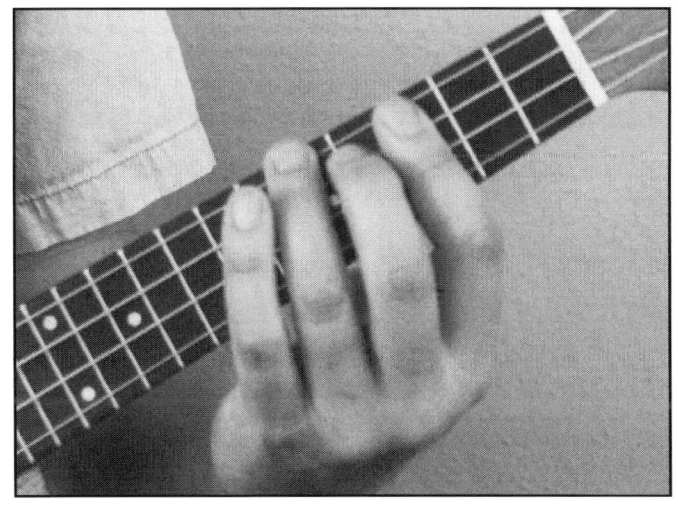
Fig.50 - C Major Barre Hand Position

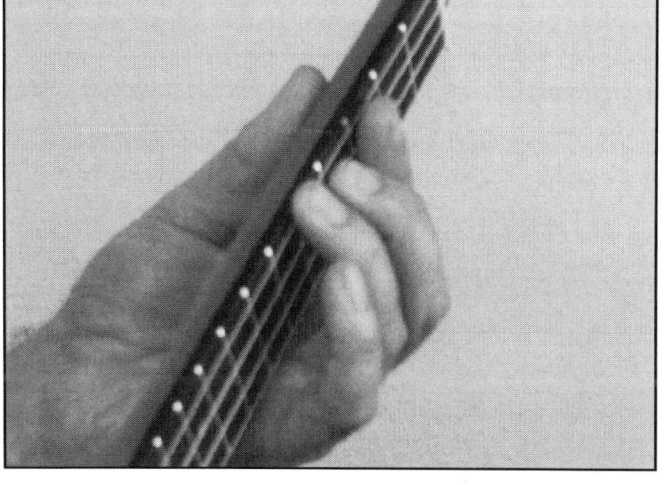
Fig.51 - C Major Barre Player's View

Give your chord a strum and then pick each note individually. Does each note ring clearly? Make little adjustments to your fretting hand to get each note sounding good. You may need to give a little arch to your 2nd and 3rd fingers so only the fingertips are touching the strings. Also, keep all your fingers as close to their frets as possible. This really helps the notes to sustain.

The ukulele isn't a very big instrument and if you have larger hands, you may find it easier to position your first finger differently. Place the tip of it on the 3rd string at the 2nd fret and then lay it down to barre both the 2nd and 1st strings. Repeat the previous instructions, now adding your 2nd and 3rd fingers. Some students find this a more relaxed hand position and relaxed hand posture is always best.

Remember that in fretboard notation, the number in the upper-left corner indicates the fret where the diagram begins. In Figure 52 below, you can see two different ways of indicating the same chord.

Notice how the 0 in the upper-left corner changes to a 3 in version on the right.

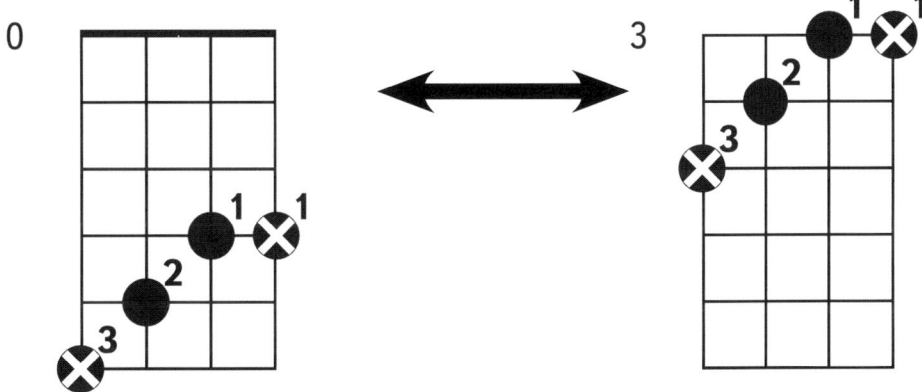
Fig.52 - Equivalent Notation of C Major

PLAYING BARRE CHORDS 35

D MAJOR BARRE CHORDS

Here is where the real magic of barre chords becomes apparent. You just learned C Major in barre chord form. To play a D Major barre chord, you will simply slide the chord up the neck (up, refers to pitch) two frets.

Hold on! Can learning a new chord be as simple as that? Moving one chord shape up the neck to a new position? In this case, yes. Have a look.

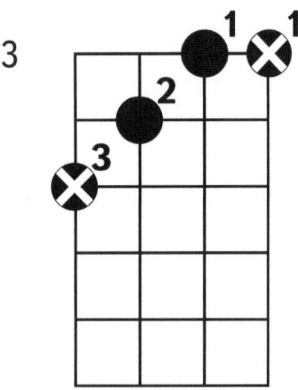

FIG.53 - C MAJOR BARRE

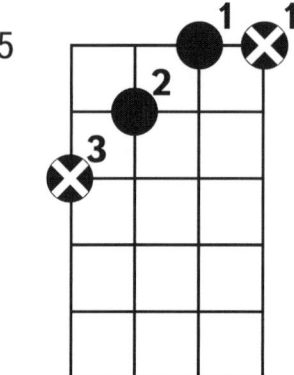

FIG.54 - D MAJOR BARRE

Notice the similarity in these two chord diagrams. In fact, the only detail that is different is the number in the upper-left corner. Simply moving the C Major chord up two frets transforms it to D Major. "Up" refers to pitch-wise or "up the neck, toward the uke body".

Just as before, start by placing your 1st finger across the first two strings, then add your 2nd finger, then your 3rd. You should end up with your 3rd finger on the 4th string at the 7th fret as in Figure 54.

Now have a look at another D Major Barre Chord. This one closely resembles the first chord you learned, C Major.

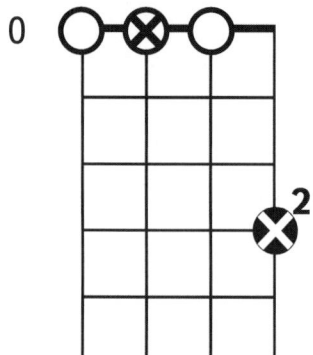

FIG.55 - C MAJOR WITH OPEN-STRINGS

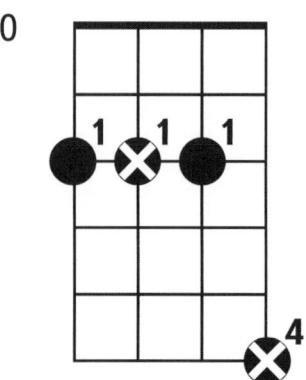

FIG.56 - D MAJOR BARRE

36 UKULELE BEGINNERS JUMPSTART: A SEEING MUSIC METHOD BOOK

Start by laying your first finger across all four strings at the 2nd fret. It's going to play notes on three of these strings.

Add your 4th or pinky finger to the group. On the 1st string at the 5th fret, add your 4th finger. Give the chord a strum. Now play each note one-at-a-time, starting with the 4th, then 3rd, then 2nd and 1st strings. Are all four notes there?

FIG.57 - D MAJOR BARRE HAND POSITION

FIG.58 - D MAJOR BARRE PLAYER'S VIEW

Keeping shapes of chords in mind helps strengthen your memory. Check out Figures 55 and 56. Close your eyes. Can you still picture both chords?

See how the open-string C Major appears very similar to the D Major barre? Three notes all on the same fret plus the 1st string note, three frets up?

This is no coincidence, but instead is one of the things that makes learning music on all stringed instruments much easier. These visual similarities make chords easy to memorize.

SEEING MUSIC

The title of this book series is Seeing Music. Do you see the similarity between the C Major barre chord and the D Major barre chord? There are many other barre chords up the neck of the ukulele that look just like the C Major barre chord and you're well on your way to knowing all of them!

Today's Assignment

Try these mini-songs using G, C and D Major chords. These chords sound terrific together and get used in many songs. Use a downward motion for each strum.

The first time you play them, use the first set of G, C and D chords below. Later try the second set, which is all barre chords.

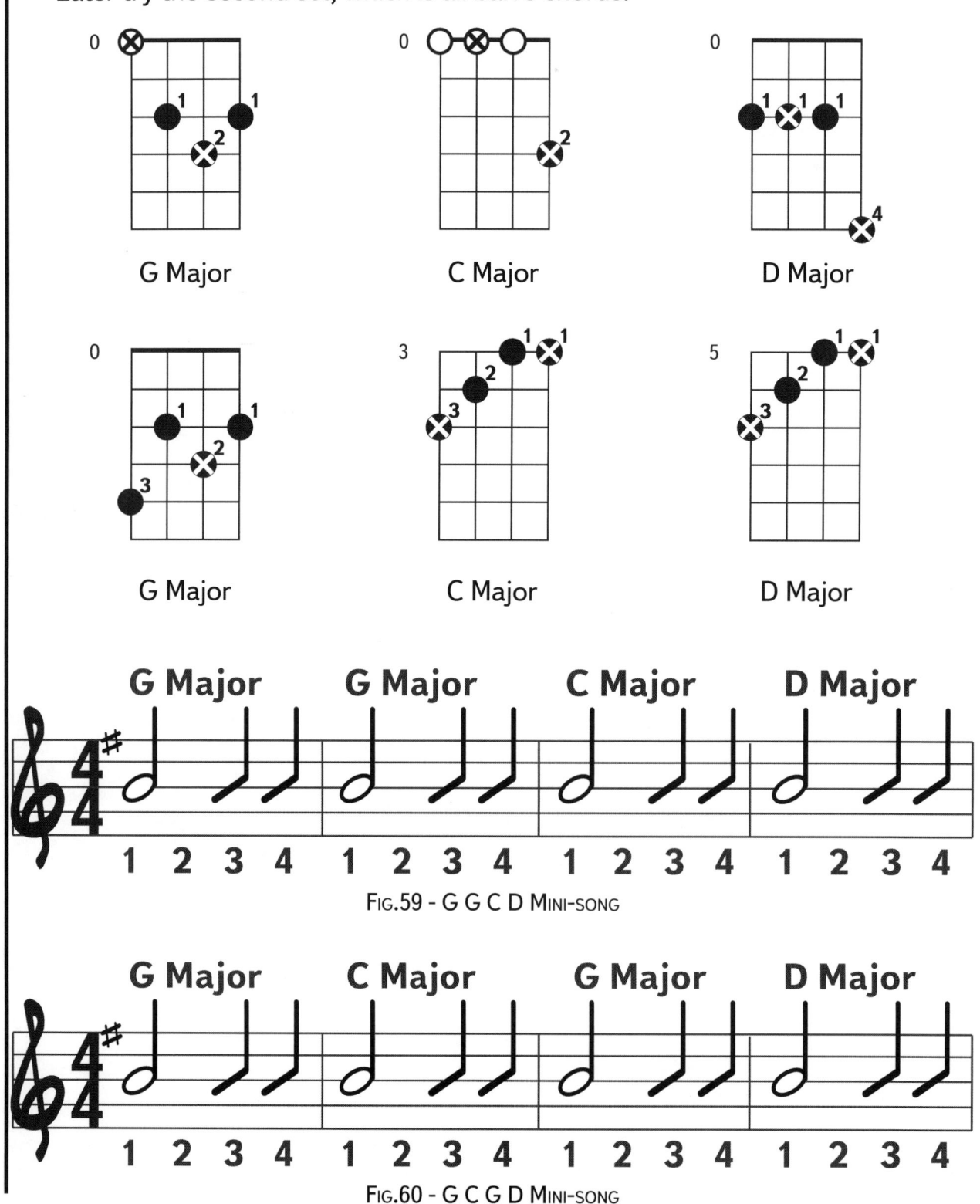

G Major   **C Major**   **D Major**

G Major   **C Major**   **D Major**

| G Major | G Major | C Major | D Major |

Fig.59 - G G C D Mini-song

| G Major | C Major | G Major | D Major |

Fig.60 - G C G D Mini-song

38 UKULELE BEGINNERS JUMPSTART: A SEEING MUSIC METHOD BOOK

DAY 6 - SCALES AND CHORDS

MILESTONE

Play the C Major scale from earlier.

Scales types (like the major scale) are defined by their combination of whole and half-steps and the note they start on (the root).

Let's start a major scale on a different note, G.

HOW TO PLAY A D MAJOR SCALE

Below are the scales for C Major and D Major. Notice how they look very similar? That's because they both use the same combination of whole and half-steps. That's not surprising because ALL major scales use the same combination of whole and half-steps.

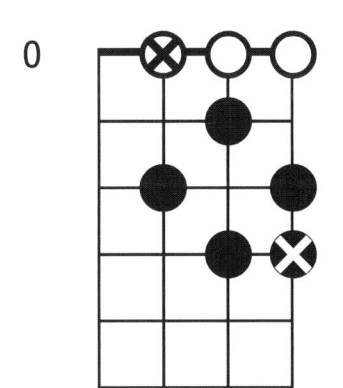

Fig.61 - C Major Scale

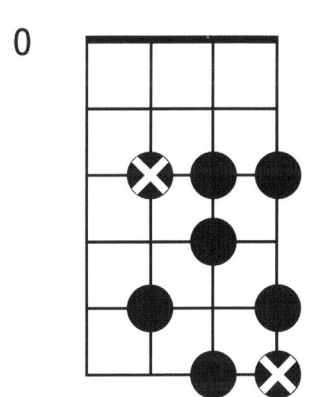

Fig.62 - D Major Scale

To play the D Major scale, start with your 1st finger. Place it on the 4th string at the 3rd fret. Follow the diagram, playing the ascending scale.

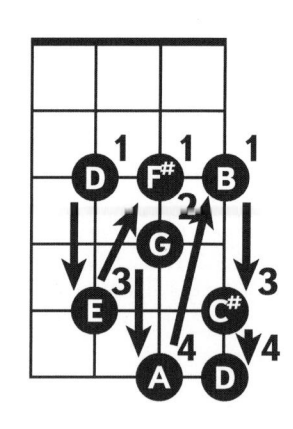

FIG.63 - D MAJOR SCALE

Here are the note names of the scale you just played.

DEF#GABC#D

FIG.64 - D MAJOR NOTE NAMES

See how the half-steps are between the 3rd and 4th, 7th and root degrees of the scale? This is just the same in the C Major scale and every other major scale.

Notice the symbol by F, the 3rd degree and C, the 7th degree? Those are sharp symbols. That means the notes are one half-step higher than F natural and C natural, respectively.

ALL ABOUT SHARPS AND FLATS

When a note is raised a half-step, we say it is *sharp*. When a note is lowered a half-step, we say it is *flat*. When it is neither, we say it is *natural*.

Here are three notes, C, C# and D. Because C sharp is also one half-step below D, we could also call it by another name: D flat. D flat and C sharp are the same note.

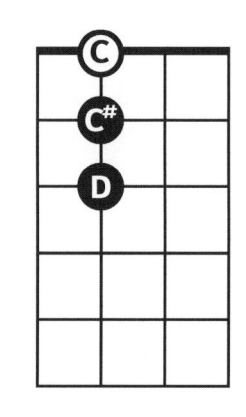

FIG.65 - C, C# AND D

40 UKULELE BEGINNERS JUMPSTART: A SEEING MUSIC METHOD BOOK

Similarly, here are F, F# and G. We could call the middle note either F sharp or G flat.

It's OK to describe a note by its natural name, such as *F natural* and *G natural*. However, for the sake of convenience, we generally just say "F" and "G".

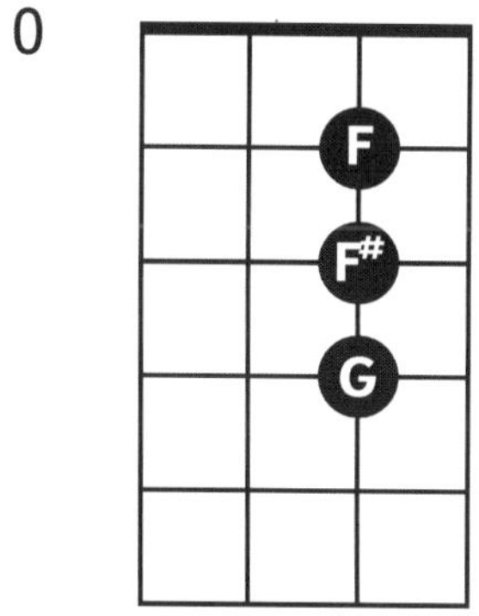

Fig.66 - F, F# and G

SEEING MUSIC

Notice how the C Major scale looks so much like the D Major scale. Even though they are made of different notes and start on different root notes, they retain a similar *visual* appearance. That fact makes them easier to memorize.

UKULELE BEGINNERS JUMPSTART

SCALES AND CHORDS 41

You're going to really like this next statement. You now know ALL three major barre chords. That's it. All of them. There's only three and you know them all. Let's review.

Play the three chords below. Notice that they use no open strings.

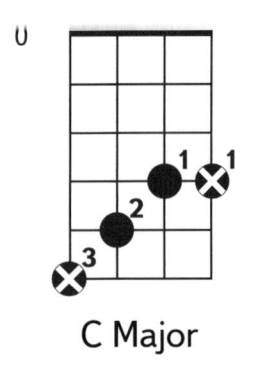

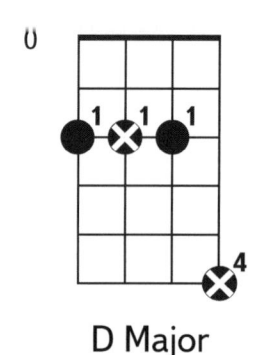

C Major

FIG.67 - C MAJOR BARRE

D Major

FIG.68 - D MAJOR BARRE

G Major

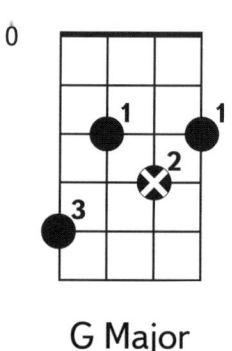

FIG.69 - G MAJOR BARRE

Every other major barre chord is based on one of these shapes, just moved up or down the neck. How cool is that?

Here's how to better remember each of these three shapes. The most important note of a chord is always its' root. In C Major, the root is C. Notice the "X" over two of the notes in this diagram. Each of them is the note C. Why are there two of them? The 1st string C doubles the 4th string C. They're actually the same note. Having two just makes the chord sound more full.

Remember this shape by taking note of the root on the 4th string.

Look at D Major. It's roots are on the 3rd and 1st strings. Remember that this shape barre chord has it's root on the 3rd string.

G Major has only one root note G and it is on the 2nd string.

So to recap, the C Major barre shape has its root on the 4th string. The D Major shape has its root on the 3rd string and the G Major shape has its root on the 2nd string.

> "Three chords, three shapes."

Three chords, three shapes.

As you practice these chords, keep in mind which notes are the root. This is the grounding that helps you keep your musical bearings.

42 UKULELE BEGINNERS JUMPSTART: A SEEING MUSIC METHOD BOOK

Today's Assignment

Here are a couple chord progressions using G and C Major chords.

In these charts, play the chord indicated four times, once for each hash mark. Watch out for the order of the chords and the changing rhythms! Each one is a little different.

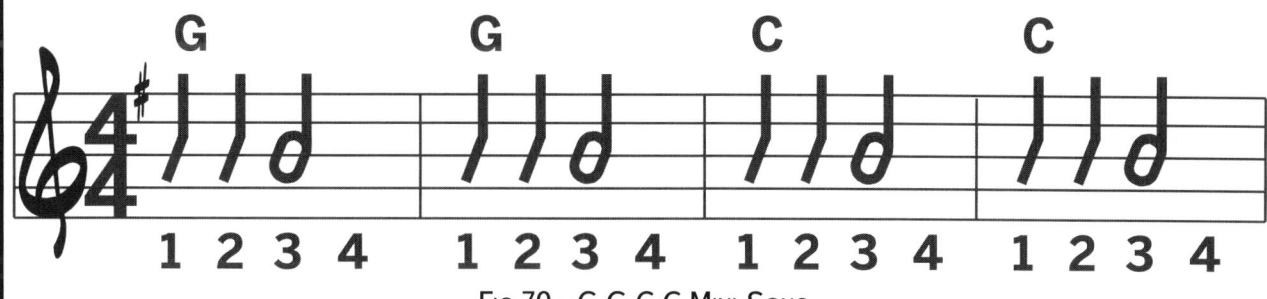

Fig. 70 - G G C C Mini-Song

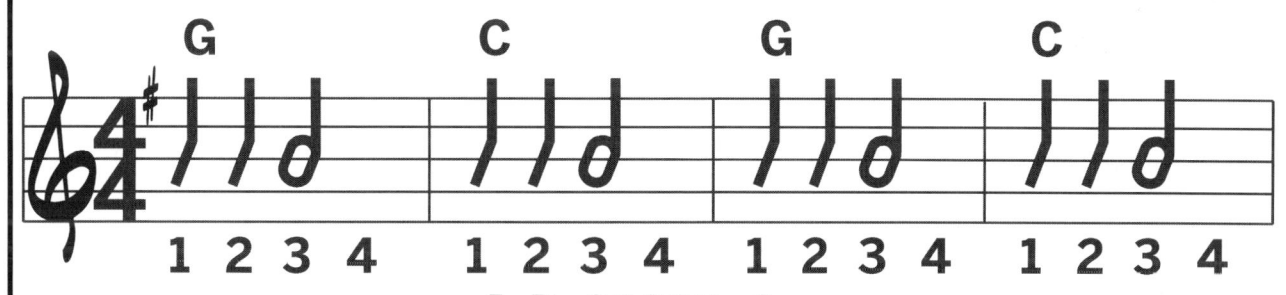

Fig. 71 - G C G C Mini-Song

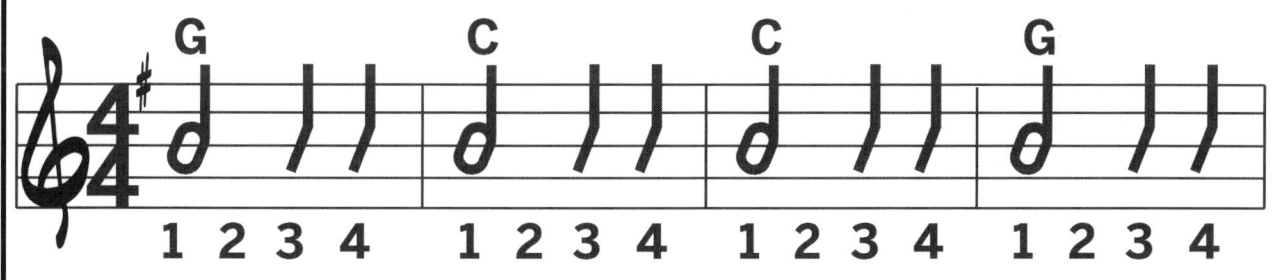

Fig. 72 - G C C G Mini-Song

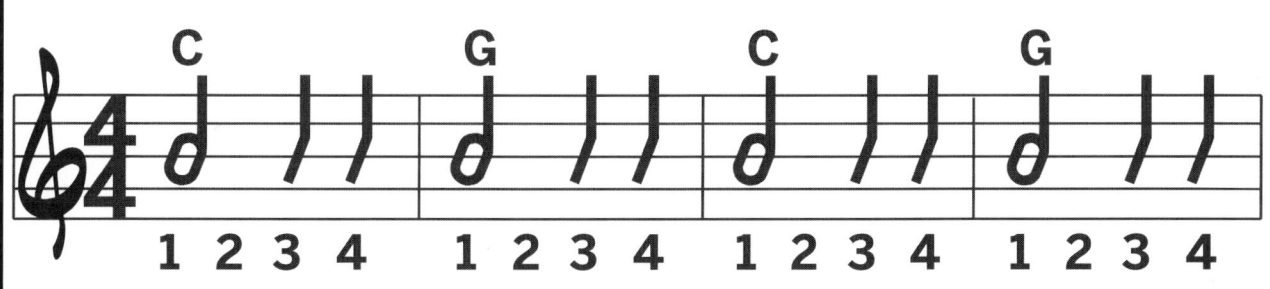

Fig. 73 - C G C G Mini-Song

SCALES AND CHORDS 43

44 UKULELE BEGINNERS JUMPSTART: A SEEING MUSIC METHOD BOOK

LEARNING YOUR FRETBOARD

One of the most important steps to playing ukulele is learning the names of the notes on the fretboard. If you know every note, everything else will be much easier to learn and play. And while the fretboard seems like a huge mess to be memorized, there are some super-easy shortcuts that will make learning much more fun.

THE FIRST 5 FRETS

Let's consider just the natural notes, those without sharps or flats. They're easiest to remember. Luckily, the C Major scale has no sharps or flats and you already know it.

Play the C Major scale now, saying the note names aloud as you do.

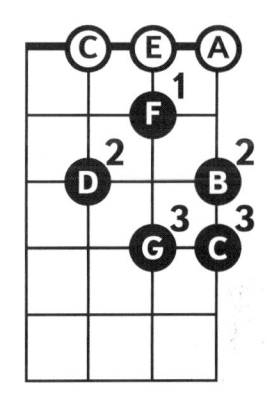

FIG.74 - C MAJOR SCALE WITH NOTE NAMES

You also know another way to play the same scale. Play it again as well, also saying the note names out loud.

Remember to start on the 3rd string C and end on the 4th string C.

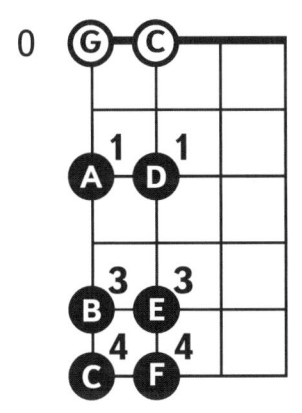

FIG.75 - C MAJOR SCALE WITH NOTE NAMES

If you're ever lost to find a note, you can always fall back on these two scales.

If you were to superimpose these two diagrams, you'd have nearly every natural note in the first 5 five frets of the ukulele. Turn the page to see them!

LEARNING YOUR FRETBOARD 45

Here are both scales superimposed. Can you see both of them? Just to complete the set, two more notes have been added on the 1st and 2nd strings at the 5th fret.

Notice how the 4th and 3rd strings have the same pattern of notes at the open-string, 2nd, 4th and 5th frets. That's handy.

Similar Fingerings

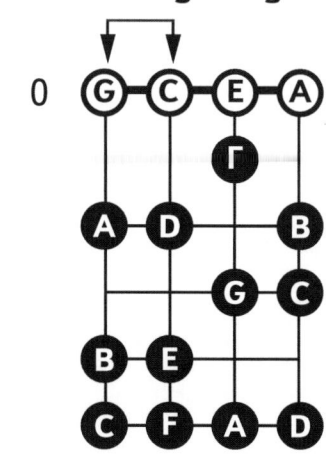

FIG.76 - NATURAL NOTES

Today's Assignment

Play all the natural notes from the two scales on the previous page, both starting on the same note, the open 3rd string C.

Once you get those memorized and can play the notes in ascending order, challenge yourself by playing these scale in descending fashion!

DAY 7 - THE WALTZ

MILESTONE

Play the G Major and C Major chords from earlier. Play the D Major barre chord, then the G Major again.

Do you hear how those three chords sound like a set that goes together?

3/4 TIME SIGNATURE

You know that many songs are in 4/4 time. This means there are four quarter-notes per measure. Another time signature is 3/4 (pronounced *three-four*).

3/4 time has three quarter notes per measure. Every waltz is in 3/4 time. That's what makes it a waltz.

SOUNDCHECK

Let's play a simple waltz using G, C and D Major.

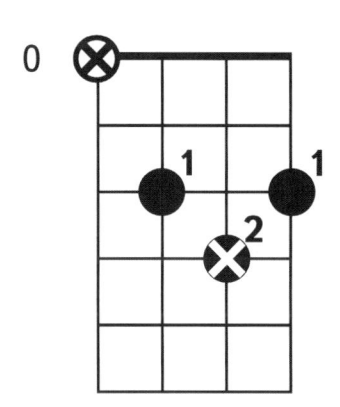

FIG.77 - G MAJOR 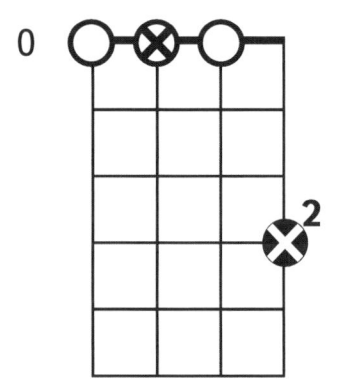   FIG.78 - C MAJOR 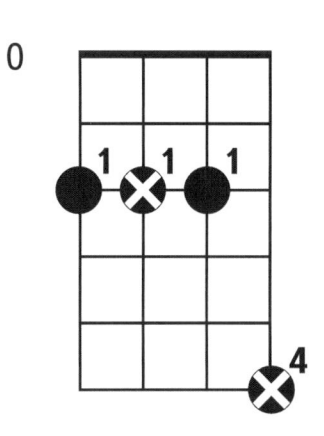   FIG.79 - D MAJOR

THE WALTZ 47

Refer to the chords above for fingerings. Play each chord with a downstroke, three times per measure.

Keep time smoothly and work to make the transitions from chord to chord smooth and seamless.

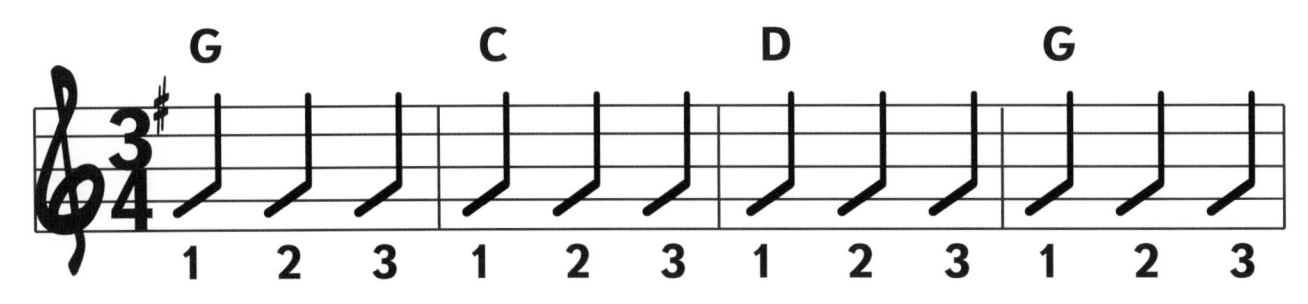

FIG.80 - Waltz in G Major

Today's Assignment

Here are a couple of mini-songs in 3/4 time using G, C and D chords. Some measures use two chords per bar so you'll be changing fingering more frequently. Use a downward motion for each strum

FIG.81 - GDC Combo Rhythms 1

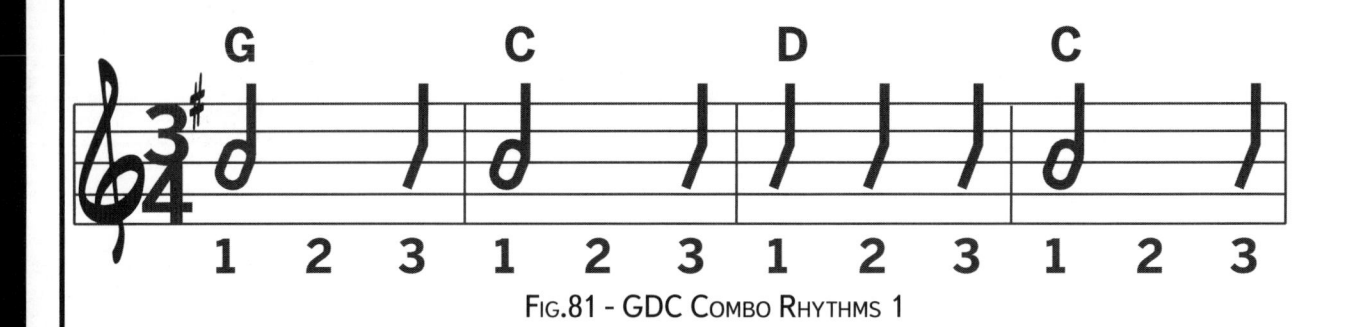

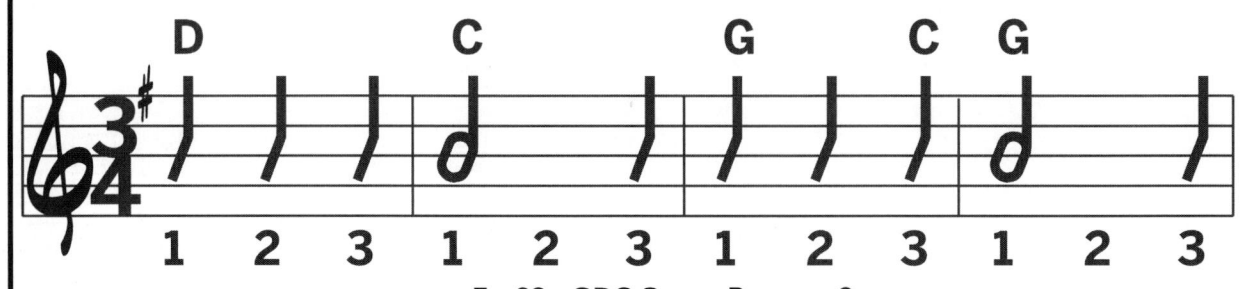

FIG.82 - GDC Combo Rhythms 2

48 UKULELE BEGINNERS JUMPSTART: A SEEING MUSIC METHOD BOOK

DAY 8 - NEW STRUMMING PATTERNS

Music is made of three elements: melody, harmony and rhythm. Melody is the singable part, generally a single note line. Harmony is all the other notes going on simultaneously that support the melody. Both melodies and harmonies have rhythm, and good rhythm helps keep things interesting.

WHAT GOES DOWN MUST COME UP

Strumming is made of two parts: the downstroke and the upstroke. Every downstroke must have an upstroke. Otherwise, your picking hand would go down toward the floor and never return, right? The upstroke brings your hand back to its starting position.

Down, up, down, up. That's what we'll work on now, because that motion is the basis for all good rhythm.

Fig.83 - Downstroke

Fig.84 - Upstroke

Work on this motion silently, at first. Following the down and upstroke symbols, move your strumming hand over the strings without actually touching any of them. This is just to get a feel for the motion.

Fig.85 - Eighth-notes

NEW STRUMMING PATTERNS 49

The rhythmic motion you're playing are eighth-notes. Just as you'd imagine, two eighth-notes equal one quarter-note. The rhythm is counted, "One-and-Two-and-Three-and-Four-and".

Now, place your left hand to fret an G Major chord. Try the same eighth-note strum. Down, then up and repeat.

Feel free to strum with either a very light pick or your index finger.

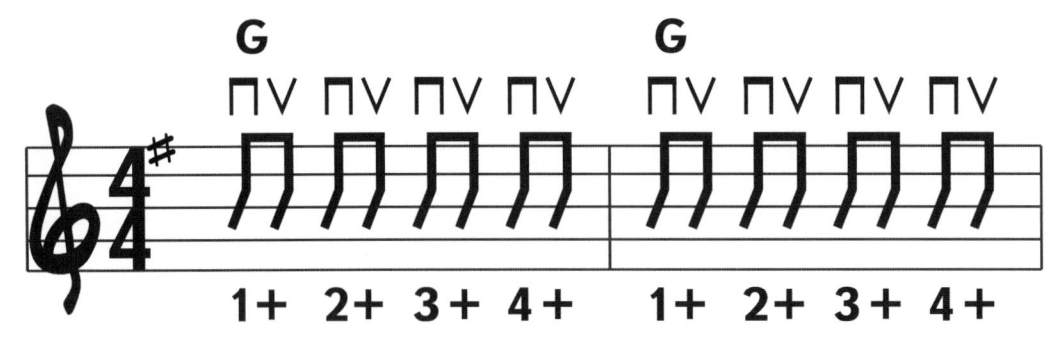

FIG.86 - UP AND DOWNSTROKES

HOW TO ADD UPSTROKES

Here's the basic downstroke pattern you've been using until now. Try it again, this time taking note of how often your hand silently makes the upstroke. A silent stroke is called a *reststroke*.

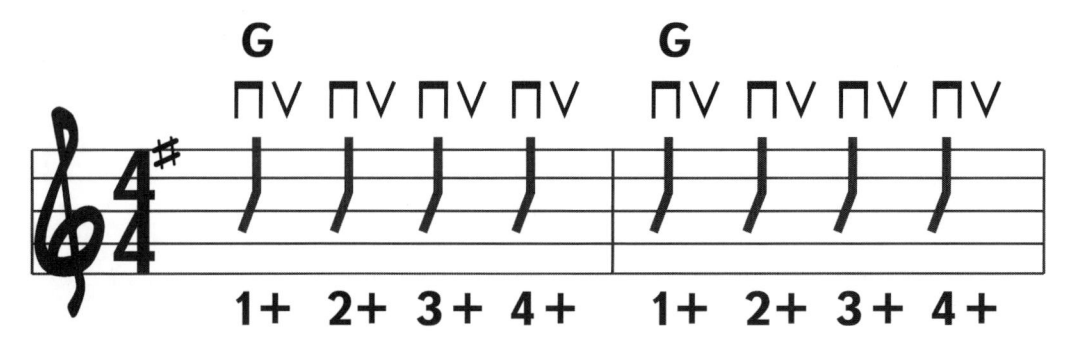

FIG.87 - DOWNSTROKES WITH RESTSTROKES

Instead of just four strokes, you were really making eight: four downward and against the strings and four silent upstrokes!

Ordinarily, downstroke and upstroke marks are only shown for the chords you should play. The reststrokes are not usually indicated.

50 UKULELE BEGINNERS JUMPSTART: A SEEING MUSIC METHOD BOOK

This is a combination rhythm. Your picking hand will continue the down, up, down, up steady movement. Just as before, sometimes you'll use silent upstrokes (reststrokes) and sometimes you'll strum the strings on the upstrokes.

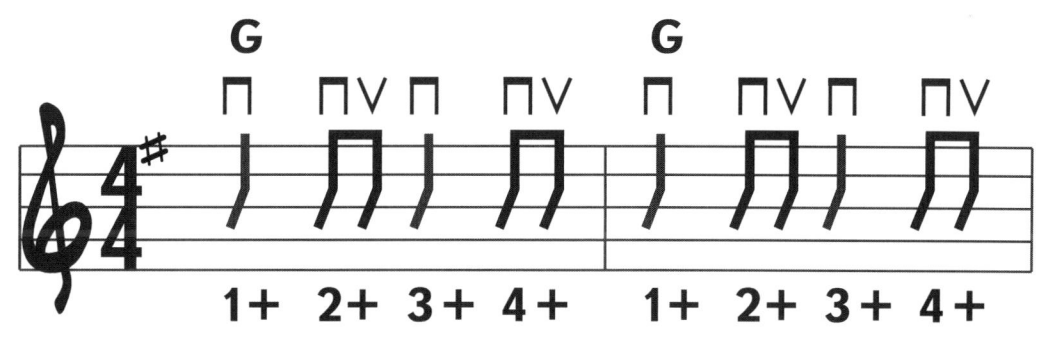

FIG.88 - COMBINATION DOWN, UP, RESTSTROKES

Here's a different combination of silent and sounded upstrokes.

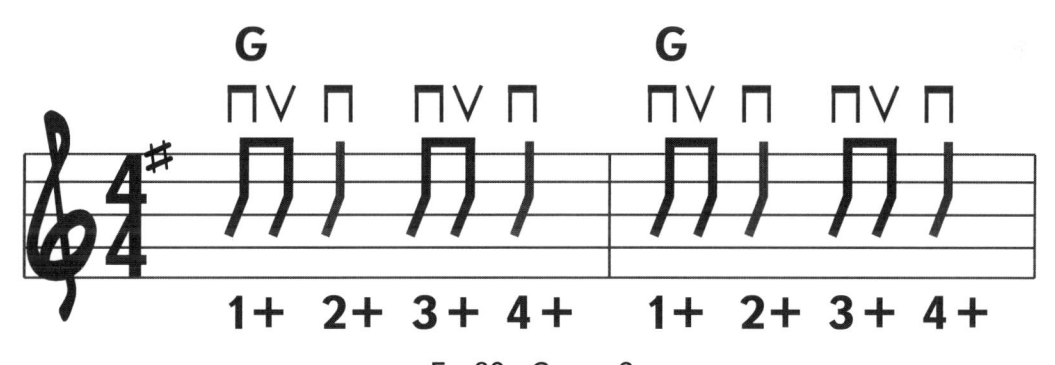

FIG.89 - COMBO 2

This is a very common rhythm used in thousands of songs.

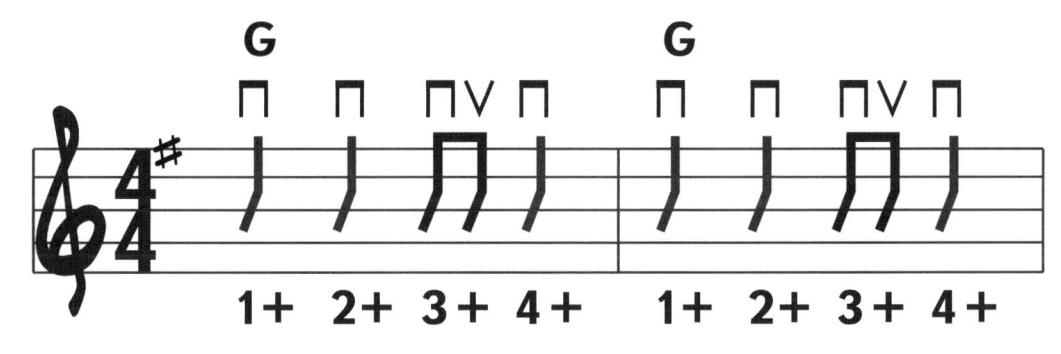

FIG.90 - COMBO 3

NEW STRUMMING PATTERNS 51

Today's Assignment

You've been playing combination rhythms using quarter- and eighth-notes. These combinations make music fantastic and much more interesting.

Start the following chord progressions slowly at first. The goal is very steady rhythm and smooth transitions between chords.

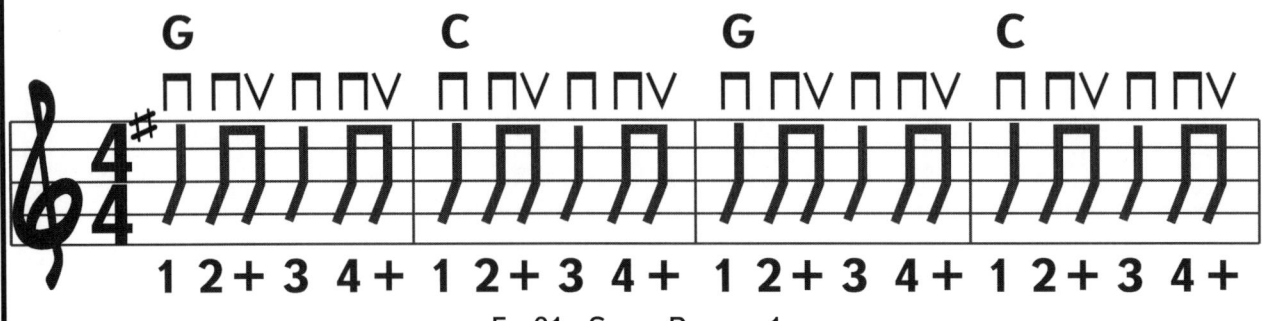

Fig.91 - Strum Rhythm 1

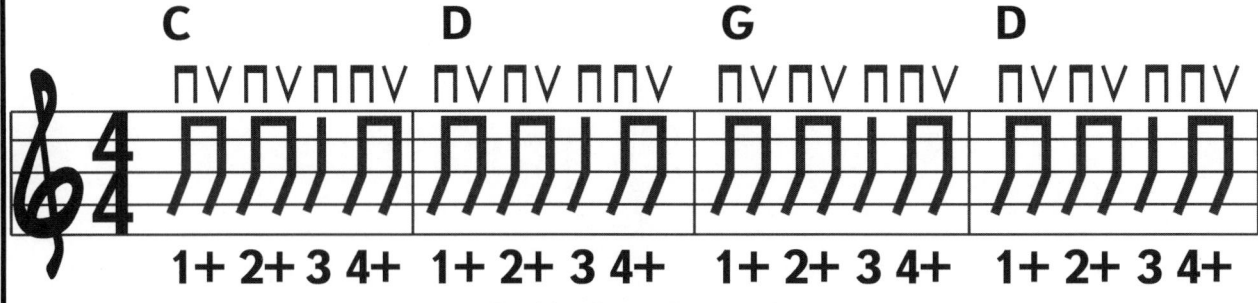

Fig.92 - Strum Rhythm 2

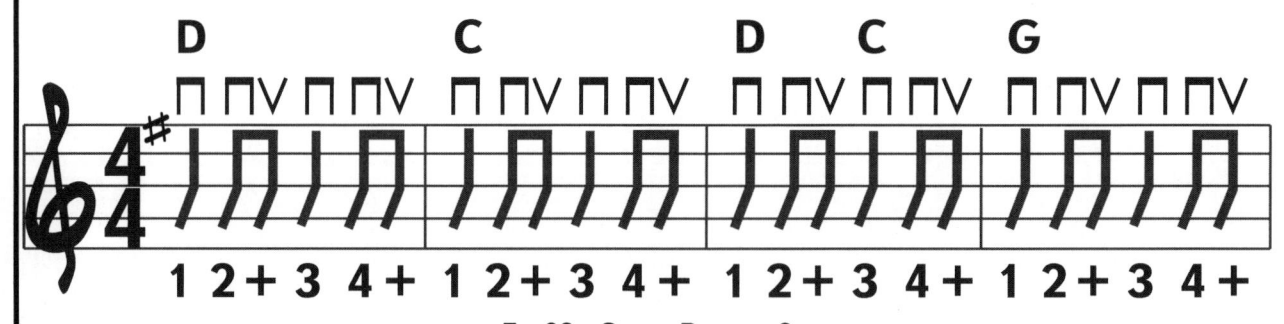

Fig.93 - Strum Rhythm 3

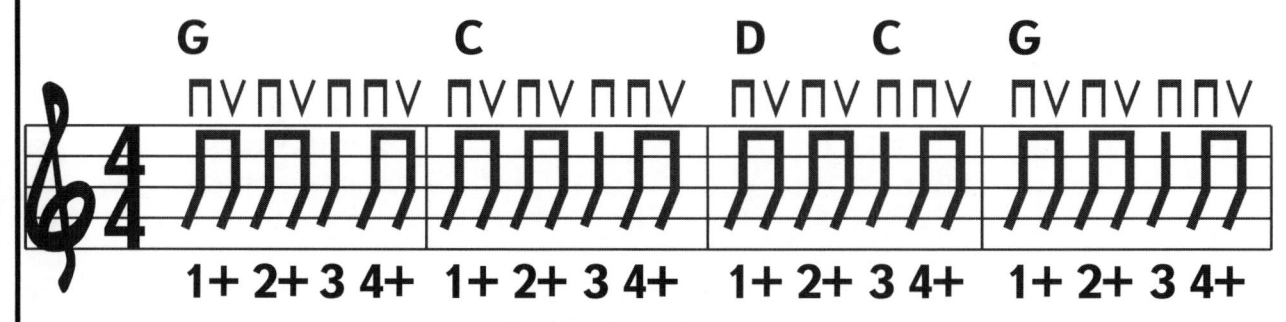

Fig.94 - Strum Rhythm 4

52 UKULELE BEGINNERS JUMPSTART: A SEEING MUSIC METHOD BOOK

DAY 9 - MORE BARRE CHORDS

MILESTONE

Play the D Major and G Major barre chords you've learned.

In this chapter, you'll see how to make new chords from those two you've already learned.

LET'S GET MOVING!

As you know, barre chords can be moved around the neck to create new chords. Here is how.

You'll remember memorizing barre chords by paying special attention to the root of each chord. There was a chord with the root on the 4th string, a chord with root on the 3rd string and one with the root on the 2nd string.

Check out your old friend, the D Major barre chord and his close relatives the E Major and F Major barre chords.

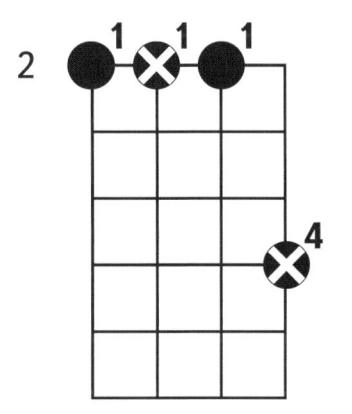

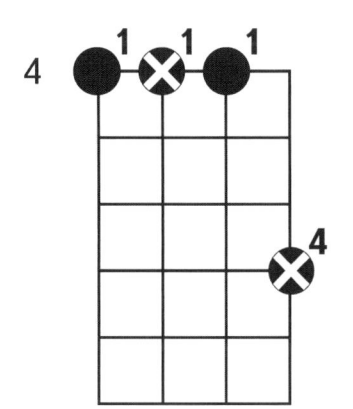

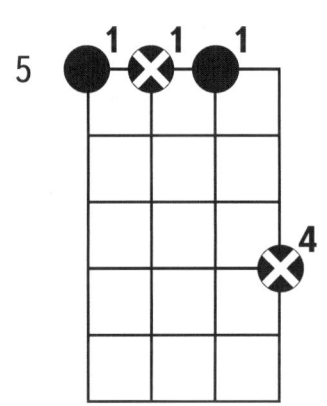

FIG.95 - D MAJOR CHORD   FIG.96 - E MAJOR BARRE CHORD   FIG.97 - F MAJOR BARRE CHORD

Notice how the only detail that changes is the fret origin number in the upper-left corner.

To play E Major, start with the D Major chord and simply slide it up two frets. To play F Major, slide it up again one more fret.

MORE BARRE CHORDS 53

Can you believe it? Because you knew the D Major barre chord, you also knew two more chords, E and F Major.

Can other barre chords be repurposed in this way? They sure can! Have a look

Recall the G Major barre chord and meet his two close relatives, A Major and B Major.

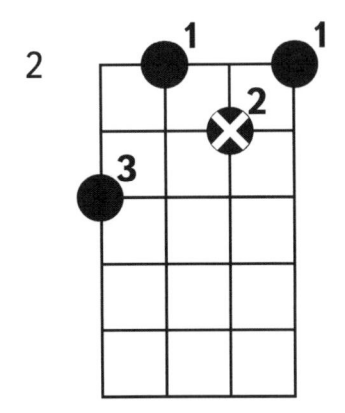

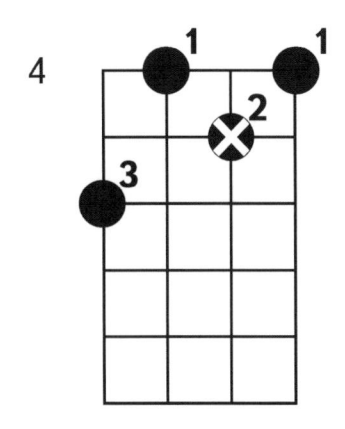

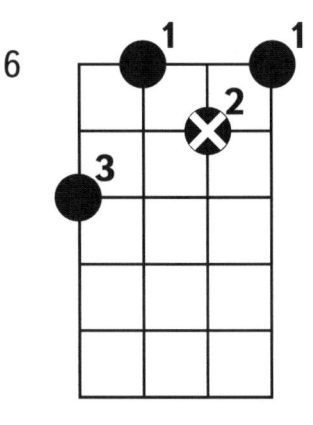

FIG.98 - G MAJOR BARRE CHORD   FIG.99 - A MAJOR BARRE CHORD   FIG.100 - B MAJOR BARRE CHORD

You've probably already noticed that the chord shape remains the same, but the number in the upper-left changes. Are barre chords really this easy? Yes!

If you can play the G Major barre chord, just slide it up two frets to create A Major. Then, slide that chord up another two frets to B Major. So simple!

Play these three chords in order and notice how easy it is to slide your fretting hand up a couple of frets to make the next new chord.

It may be simple process but it sounds great, doesn't it?

A Universe of Scales is Waiting for You

Learn scales and modes with multiple fingerings and tons of exercises.

seeingmusicbooks.com

There's one more barre chord shape that can be moved around and you've already seen it used for C Major in Figure 101.

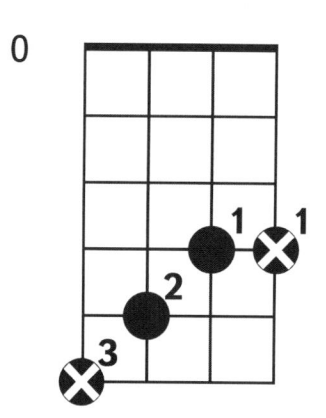

FIG.101 - C MAJOR BARRE CHORD

Below is that same C Major chord, rewritten with the fretboard diagram starting at the 3rd fret.

To repurpose it into other chords, start by playing C Major barre and this time slide the chord *down*. Slide down one fret as in Figure 103 to play B Major.

You can see that the shape of A Major is just the same as B and C Major. But since it uses open-strings, you'll need to adjust your fingering a bit.

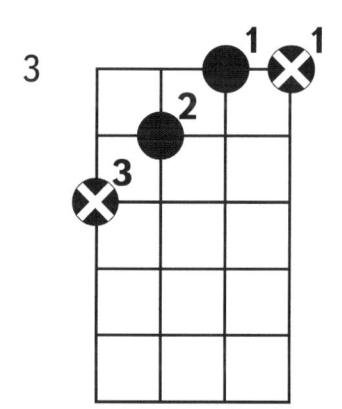

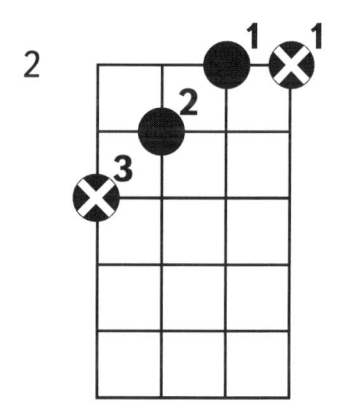

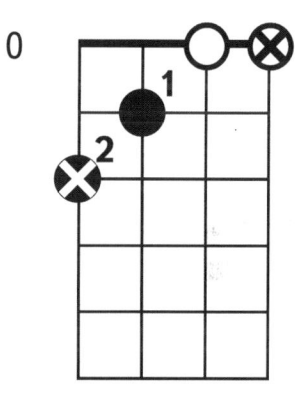

FIG.102 - C MAJOR BARRE CHORD   FIG.103 - B MAJOR BARRE CHORD   FIG.104 - A MAJOR CHORD

You seen a whole bunch of major chords. In fact, you've seen A, B, C, D, E, F and G Major. And in many cases, you now know a couple of different ways to play those chords. Wow!

When playing ukulele, it's sometimes helpful to have a couple of options for how to finger or *voice* a chord. You may prefer one fingering to another because of the sound or just because it's more convenient to transition between the given chords of a song.

In the next chapter, you'll find a whole new world of chords that sound great amidst major chords: minor chords.

MORE BARRE CHORDS

It's MUCH more than
just a dictionary.
Fast Reference for Many Scales and Modes
Organized by Root and Scale Type
Multiple Fingerings for Each Scale
Learn to Spell Any Scale
Learn Modes, Pentatonics and More
SEEING MUSIC
METHOD BOOKS
GUITAR
SCALES
ENCYCLOPEDIA
Fast Reference for the Scales You Need in Every Key
ANDY SCHNEIDER
BEGINNER TO ADVANCED
See more music at
SeeingMusicBooks.com
SEEING MUSIC
METHOD BOOKS

DAY 10 - MINOR CHORDS

||||||||||||||||||||||||||||||||||||||||||||||||||||||||||||||||||||||
MILESTONE

Play the G, C and F Major open-string chords from Figures.

Every chord has a major version and a minor version.
||||||||||||||||||||||||||||||||||||||||||||||||||||||||||||||||||||||

CHANGE MAJOR TO MINOR

As if with a magic wand, any chord can be changed into minor. Wouldn't that be nice? To have a magic music wand? Well, you do! Check this out.

Play the three note chord at right. It's a shortened version of the G Major barre chord you've already learned. The 1st string note has been left off but it will still sound fine.

Now try the G Minor chord below. Start building the chord from the 4th string. Place your 2nd finger at the 3rd fret. Then add your 1st finger, then 3rd.

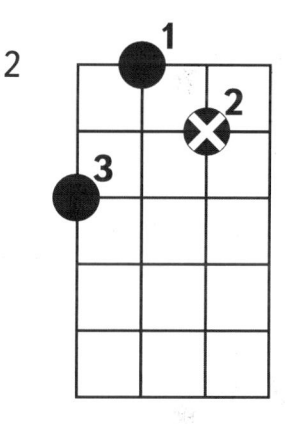

FIG.105 - G MAJOR CHORD

See how there is only one note difference between these two chords? The note on the 4th string has moved down one fret. That small change turns this major chord into a minor chord. Play the G Minor version and notice the big difference in sound between it and G Major.

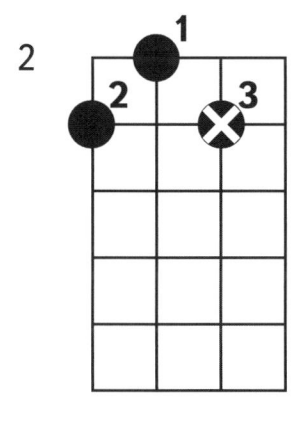

FIG.106 - G MINOR CHORD

Generally, minor chords are used in songwriting to impart a sad feeling. Major chords, a happy feeling. Isn't it funny how changing just one note can do that?

FIG. 107 - G MINOR HAND POSITION

FIG. 108 - G MINOR PLAYER'S VIEW

MORE MAGIC MINOR

Just as one note change converted G Major to G Minor, one note changes D Major to D Minor. Here again is the shortened version of a chord you know, D Major.

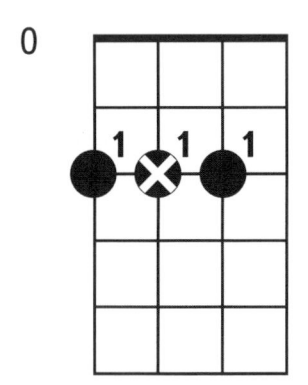

FIG. 109 - D MAJOR CHORD

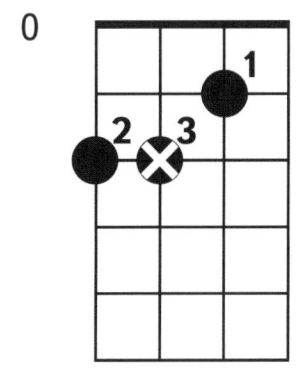

FIG. 110 - D MINOR CHORD

Heads up! You'll need to use a very different fingering to reach D Minor. Notice the fingerings in the diagram.

Remember there are three major barre chord shapes. Let's see if the third barre chord shape can also be made into a minor barre chord.

58 UKULELE BEGINNERS JUMPSTART: A SEEING MUSIC METHOD BOOK

FIG.111 - D MINOR HAND POSITION

FIG.112 - D MINOR PLAYER'S VIEW

This is a shortened version of C Major you've already seen using all four strings. Presto! Watch it turn into a minor chord.

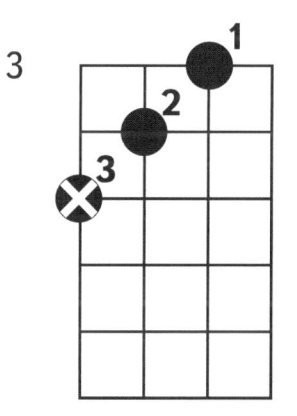

FIG.113 - C MAJOR CHORD

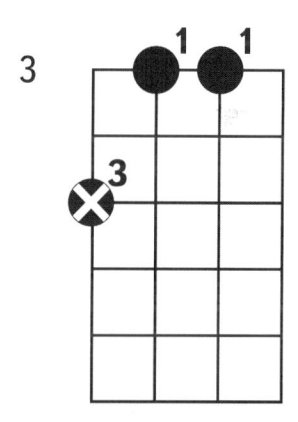

FIG.114 - C MINOR CHORD

FIG.115 - C MINOR HAND POSITION

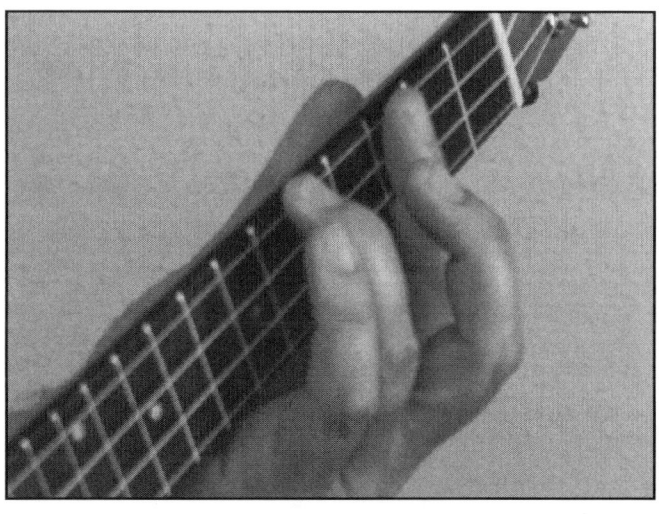

FIG.116 - C MINOR PLAYER'S VIEW

Wow, now you also know a whole bunch of minor chords! That will come in handy when learning songs in the future. It's common for songwriters to blend combinations of major and minor chords together in a song to create an interesting balance.

MINOR CHORDS 59

PUTTING CHORD FLAVORS TOGETHER

Good music is like good cooking. It's about finding combinations of flavors that are interesting and go together well. Major and minor chords sound great together and create interesting harmonies because of their different flavors.

One chord combination that sounds terrific is F Major and D Minor. Another is C Major and A Minor. And these combinations appear in lots of songs, so they are worth knowing. You've already learned D Minor. Before seeing A Minor, have a look at some of the ways it might appear in sheet music.

Note: There are many ways to write the chord symbol for the same chord. Here are some of the ways minor chords are indicated.

$$A \text{ min} = A^- = a$$

FIG.117 - MINOR KEY NAMING CONVENTIONS

These types of notations work for any minor chord. Just substitute the letter of the root note and you might see a chord called "D min" or "d".

Here again is your old pal, A Major. It's an easy chord to play since it uses two open-strings. It's even easier to play the minor version. It has three open-strings!

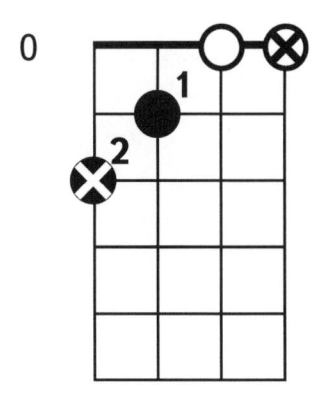

FIG.118 - A MAJOR CHORD

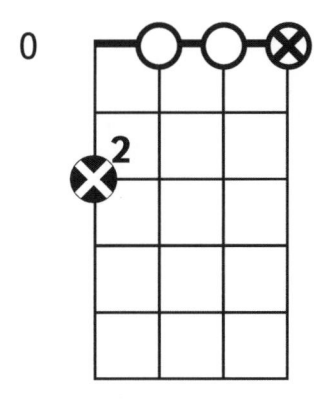

FIG.119 - A MINOR CHORD

60 UKULELE BEGINNERS JUMPSTART: A SEEING MUSIC METHOD BOOK

Today's Assignment

Try these progressions of chords, taking note of the different rhythms and time signatures. Notice the new fingering of C Major. Using your 4th finger here will free up your 2nd finger to transition to A Minor smoothly.

Start the following chord progressions slowly at first. The goal is very steady rhythm and smooth transitions between chords, not high-speed!

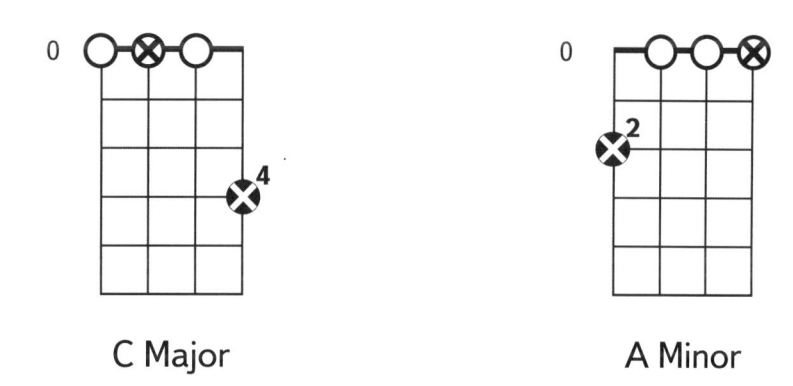

C Major

A Minor

FIG.120 - C MAJOR - A MINOR PROGRESSION

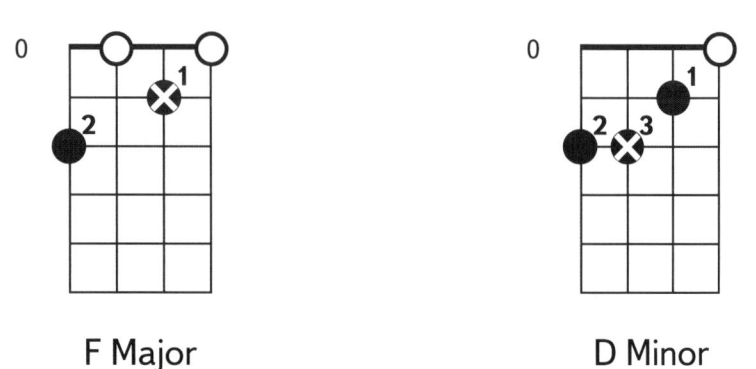

F Major

D Minor

FIG.121 - F MAJOR - D MINOR PROGRESSION

MINOR CHORDS

ASSIGNMENT

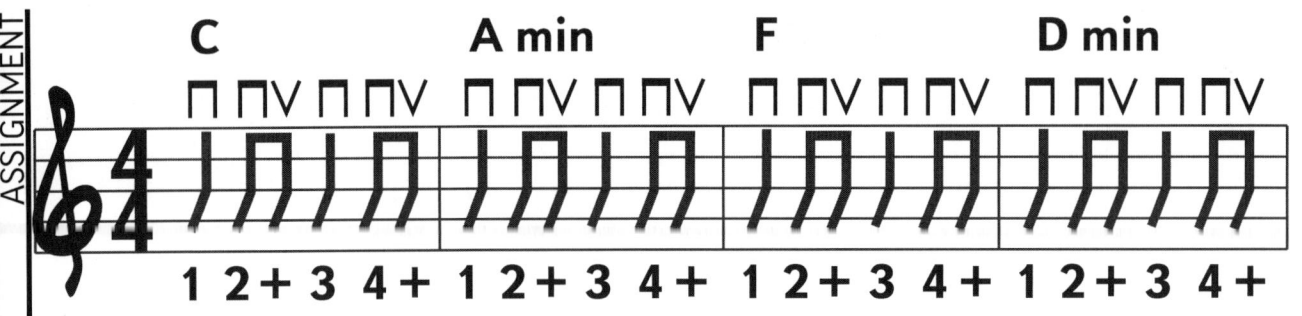

C	A min	F	D min
⊓ ⊓V ⊓ ⊓V	⊓ ⊓V ⊓ ⊓V	⊓ ⊓V ⊓ ⊓V	⊓ ⊓V ⊓ ⊓V

1 2 + 3 4 + 1 2 + 3 4 + 1 2 + 3 4 + 1 2 + 3 4 +

Fig.122 - Mini-Song in C Major

Below is a very common 4-chord progression that gets used quite often. See if it sounds familiar.

What's most important here is the order of the chords. Most any rhythm will sound fine with them. First learn the rhythm indicated, then try making up your own strumming pattern using the same chords.

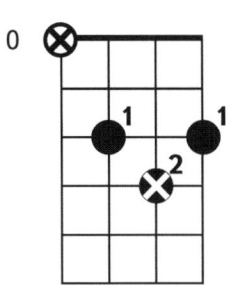

G Major

In the last measure, use the G Major voicing at right.

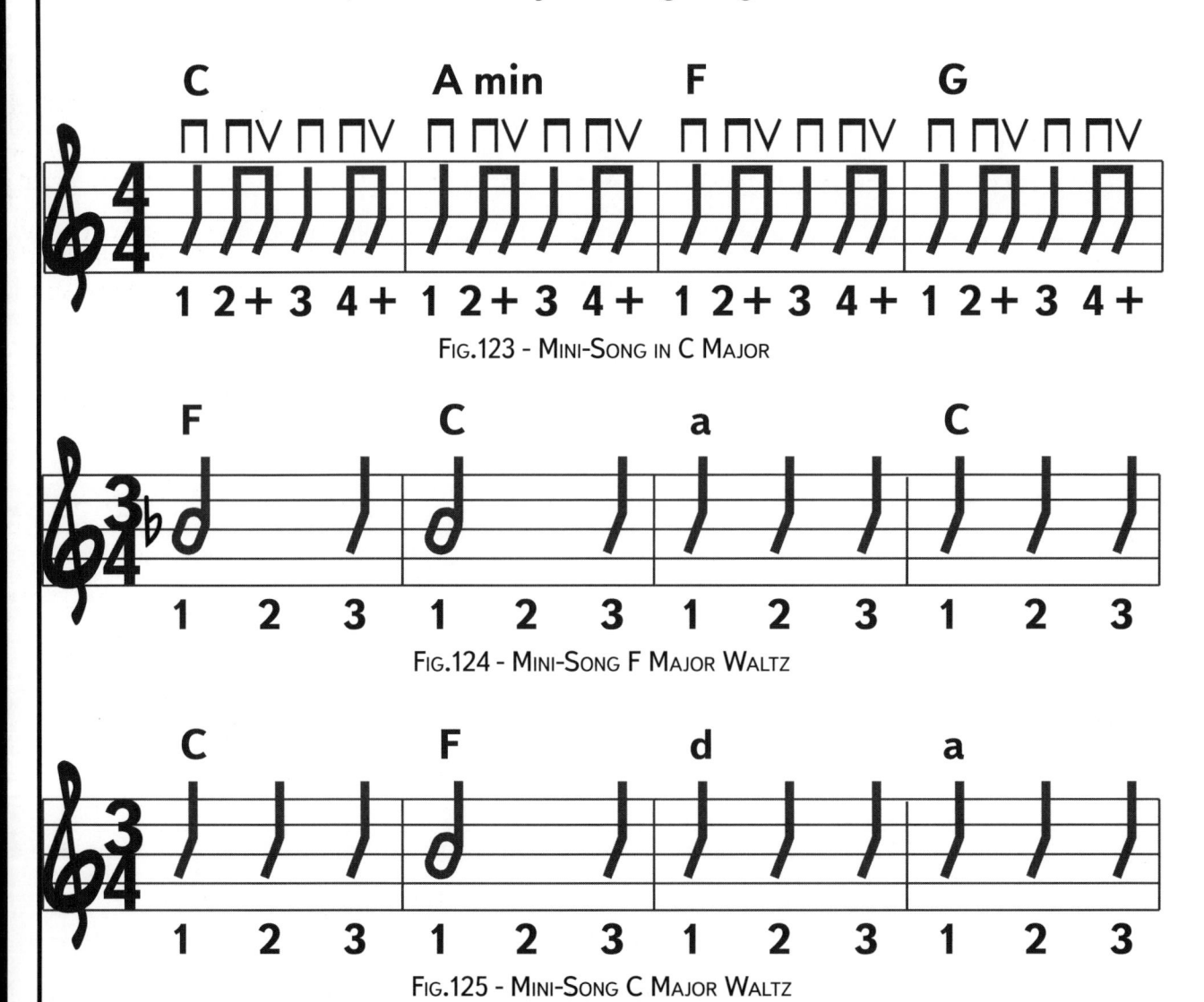

C	A min	F	G
⊓ ⊓V ⊓ ⊓V	⊓ ⊓V ⊓ ⊓V	⊓ ⊓V ⊓ ⊓V	⊓ ⊓V ⊓ ⊓V

1 2 + 3 4 + 1 2 + 3 4 + 1 2 + 3 4 + 1 2 + 3 4 +

Fig.123 - Mini-Song in C Major

F	C	a	C

1 2 3 1 2 3 1 2 3 1 2 3

Fig.124 - Mini-Song F Major Waltz

C	F	d	a

1 2 3 1 2 3 1 2 3 1 2 3

Fig.125 - Mini-Song C Major Waltz

DAY 11 - ALL ABOUT 7TH CHORDS

MILESTONE

The ukulele is a colorful instrument. It has a unique voice and tuning which lends itself to many colorful chords.

You already know many major and minor chords. There are other types of chords too which bring even more variety and flavor to music. And, they are based upon the chords you already know.

EXTENDED CHORDS ADD COLOR

The chords you've seen until now have been basic major and minor chords. That is, they each are made of three notes. Sometimes on the ukulele one of those notes is doubled so each of the four strings has a note to play, but they were really just three-note groupings.

Those chords sound great and are common to all kinds of music. The have a basic flavor that works well. But there exist a whole bunch of ways those chords can be embellished to bring a whole new harmonic interest.

These chords are called *extended chords* and they are built by extending the three-note groupings of standard major and minor chords.

The types of extended chords you'll see here are all varieties of 7th chords. They're called 7th chords because they add the 7th note of the scale on which they're based.

> *Chords are like cars. There are several basic models that work all the time.*
>
> *Then there are some upgrades and added features that customize them.*
>
> *That's what extending chords to include 7ths does. It customizes the basic chord and makes it unique.*

ALL ABOUT 7TH CHORDS 63

DOMINANT 7TH CHORDS

As a first example, recall the first chord you learned in this book: C Major. By changing one note this chord becomes "C Dominant 7" or just "C7".

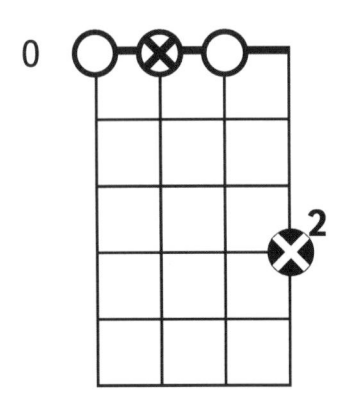

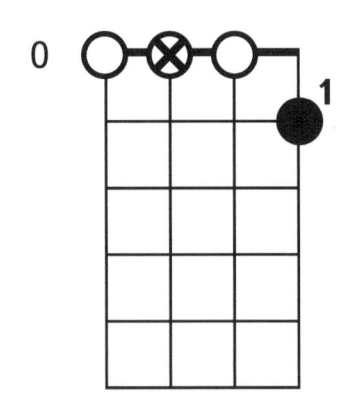

Fig.126 - C Major Chord

Fig.127 - C7 Chord

Do you hear the big difference made by changing just one note? Ukulele music uses this chord all the time because it sounds great and is super fun to play!

Fig.128 - C7 Hand Position

Fig.129 - C7 Player's View

64 UKULELE BEGINNERS JUMPSTART: A SEEING MUSIC METHOD BOOK

Here is the familiar F Major chord, turning into an F7 dominant chord.

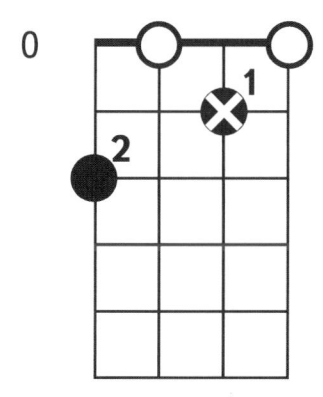

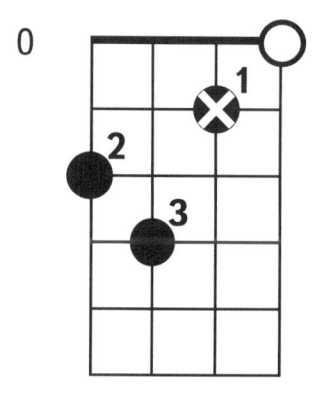

FIG.130 - F MAJOR CHORD

FIG.131 - F7 CHORD

Do you see the three notes these chords have in common? Play both of them and listen to the subtle differences between them.

FIG.132 - F7 HAND POSITION

FIG.133 - F7 PLAYER'S VIEW

ALL ABOUT 7TH CHORDS 65

This next chord is built by changing the D Major Barre chord into a D7 Barre. Check it out.

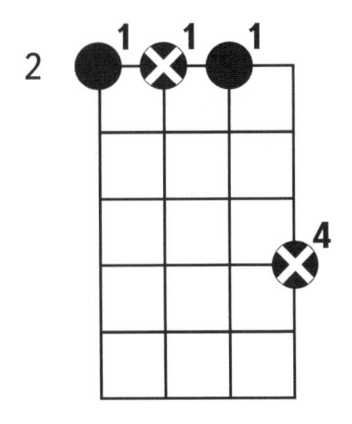

FIG.134 - D Major Chord

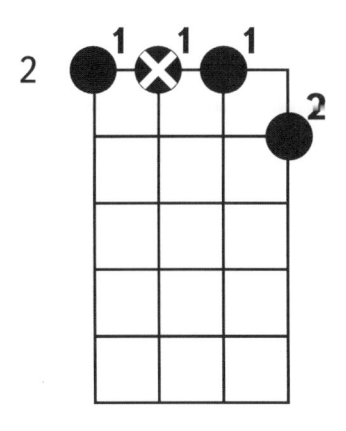

FIG.135 - D7 Chord

FIG.136 - D7 Hand Position

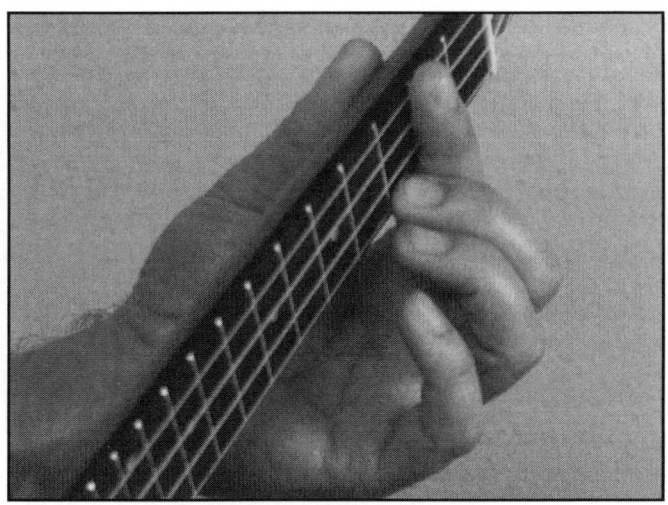

FIG.137 - D7 Player's View

MINOR 7TH CHORDS

As you might expect, minor 7th chords are built by extending minor chords. They also have a familiar visual shape.

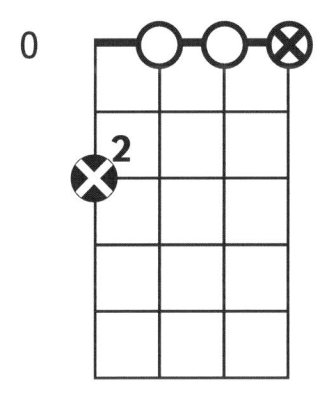

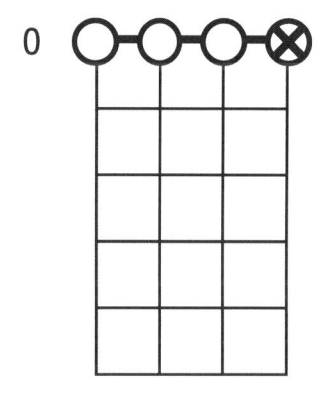

FIG.138 - A Minor Chord

FIG.139 - Amin7 Chord

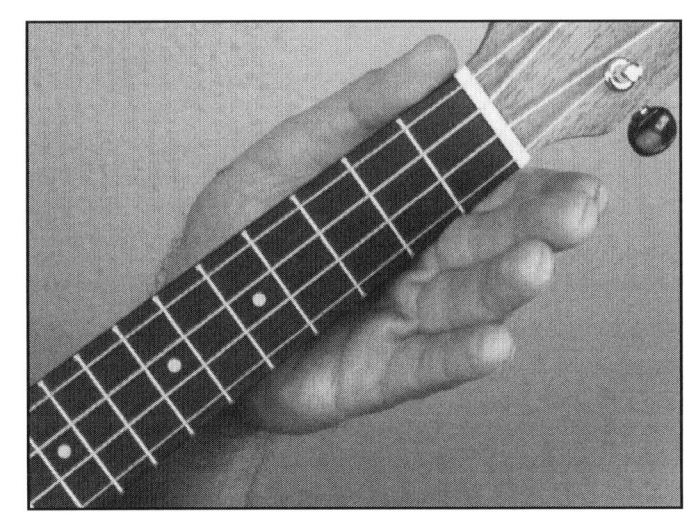

FIG.140 - Amin7 Hand Position

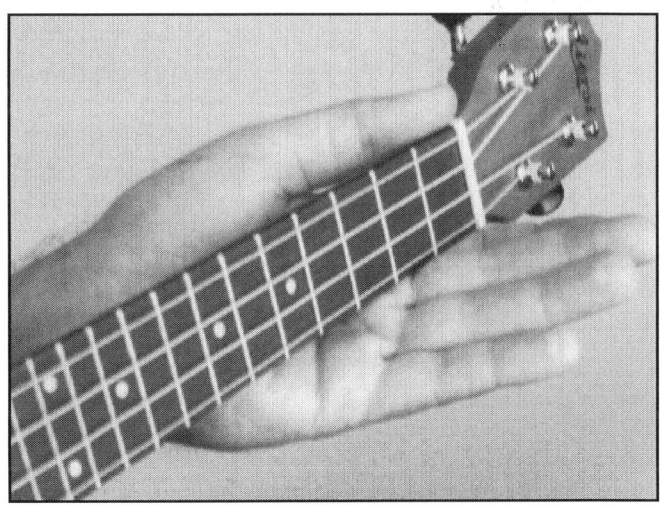

FIG.141 - Amin7 Player's View

Definitely the easiest chord in the whole ukulele universe, A Minor7 requires no fretting fingers and still sounds great!.

ALL ABOUT 7TH CHORDS 67

MAJOR 7TH CHORDS

Not unlike dominant 7th chords, major 7th chords are also built from basic major chords. They have a bright, cheerful sound.

Have a look at these major chords becoming major 7th chords and then listen to the big difference made by changing just one note.

While you haven't played these major chords before, you have played their barre chords. The E flat Major barre should look a lot like the D Major barre on the previous page. The B flat Major barre will remind you of the C Major barre you learned earlier.

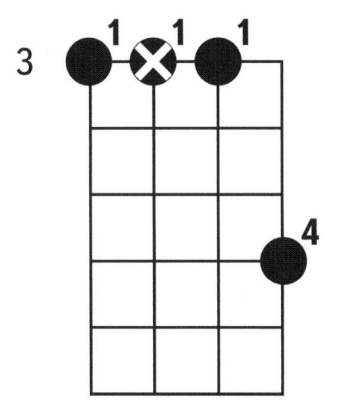

FIG.142 - E FLAT MAJOR CHORD

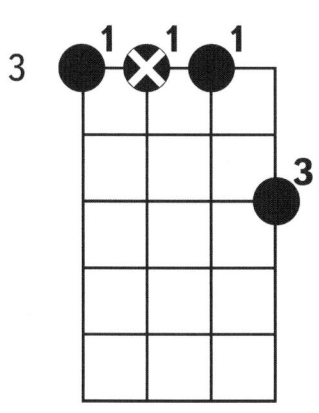

FIG.143 - E FLAT MAJOR7 CHORD

FIG.144 - E FLAT MAJOR 7 HAND POSITION

FIG.145 - E FLAT MAJOR 7 PLAYER'S VIEW

68 UKULELE BEGINNERS JUMPSTART: A SEEING MUSIC METHOD BOOK

Fig.146 - B flat Major Chord

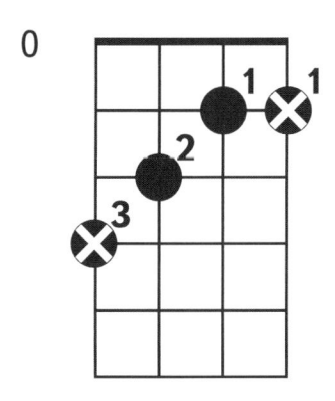

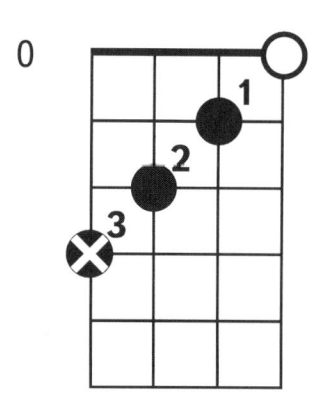

Fig.147 - B flat Major7 Chord

One advantage to learning music using a visual system is that it makes learning new chords and concepts much easier. If you can picture the basic major chord, it makes it easier to remember the major 7th version.

Fig.148 - B flat Major 7 Hand Position

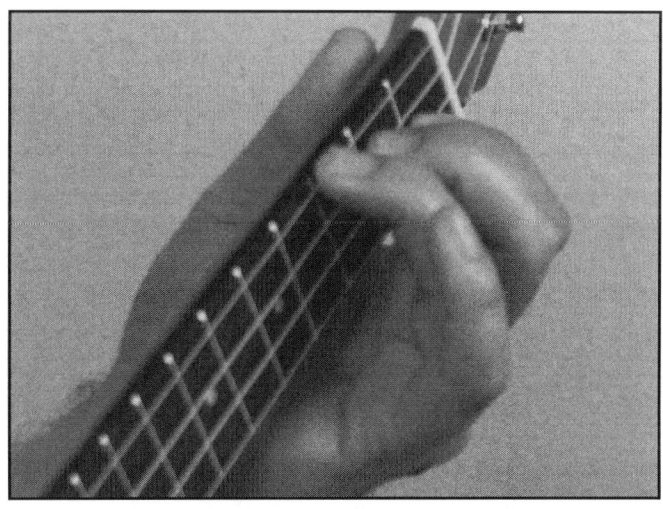

Fig.149 - B flat Major 7 Player's View

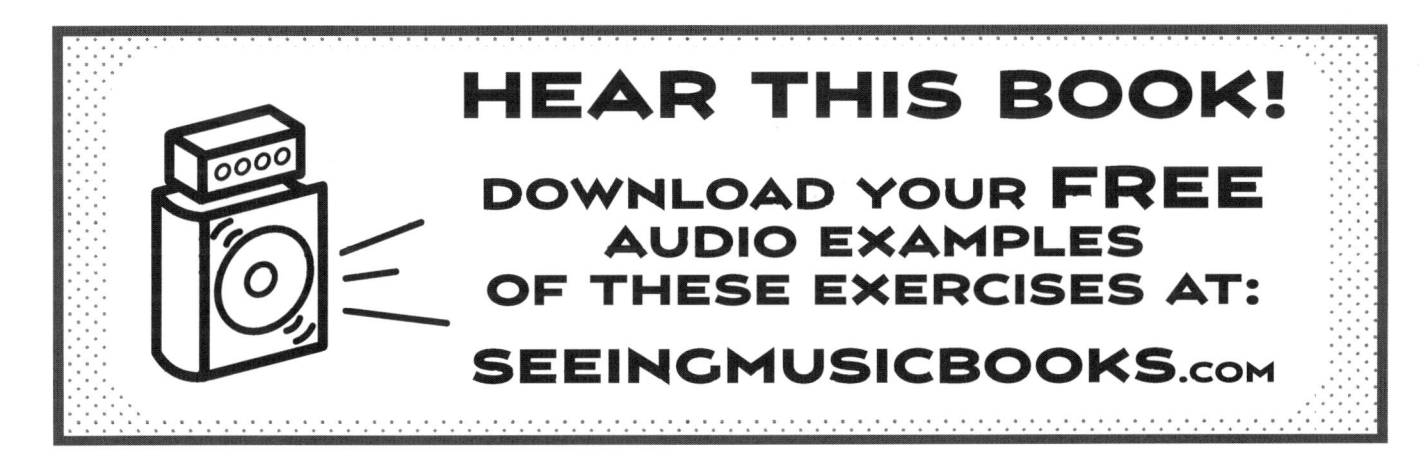

HEAR THIS BOOK!
DOWNLOAD YOUR **FREE** AUDIO EXAMPLES OF THESE EXERCISES AT:
SEEINGMUSICBOOKS.COM

ALL ABOUT 7TH CHORDS

ASSIGNMENT

Today's Assignment

Try these progressions of 7th chords, taking note of the different rhythms.

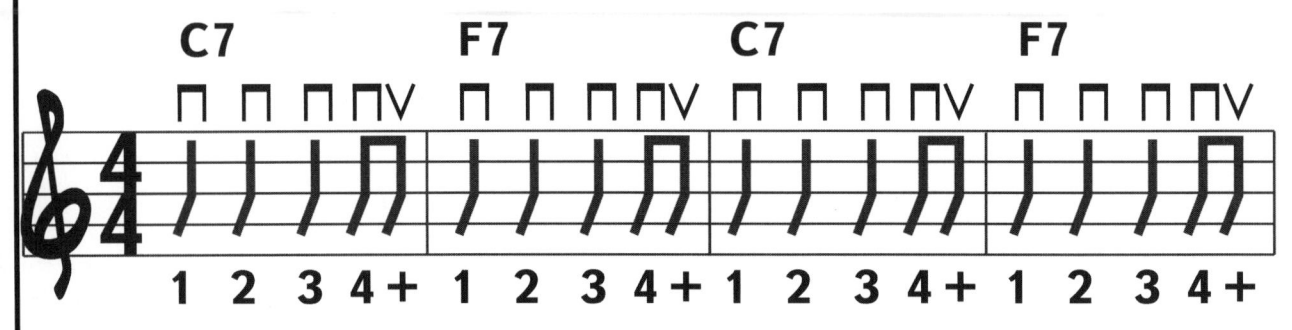

FIG.150 - MINI-SONG USING DOMINANT 7TH CHORDS

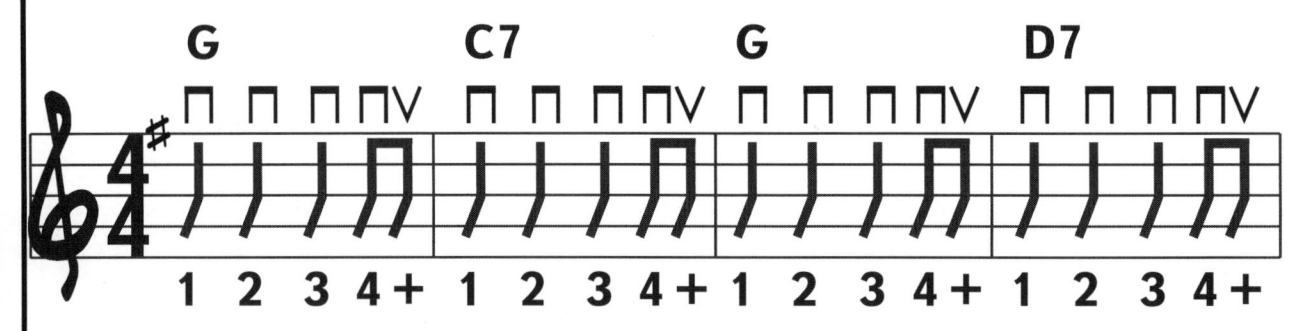

FIG.151 - MINI-SONG USING DOMINANT 7TH CHORDS

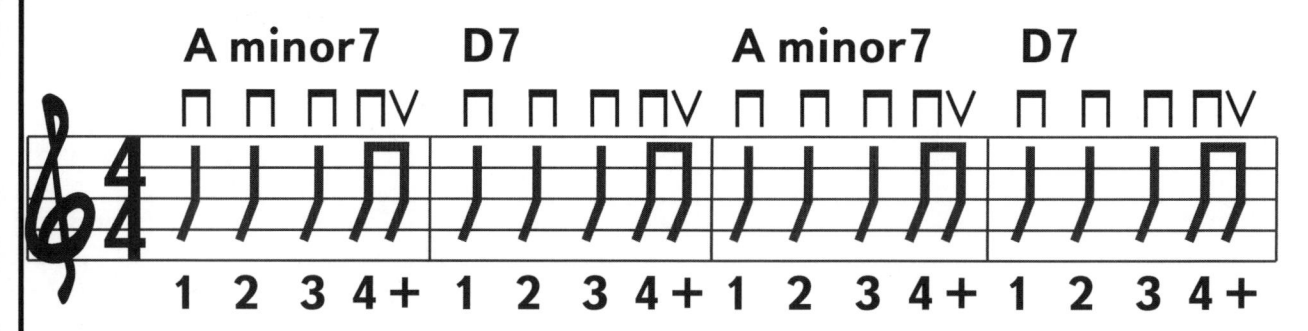

FIG.152 - MINI-SONG USING DIFFERENT 7TH CHORD TYPES

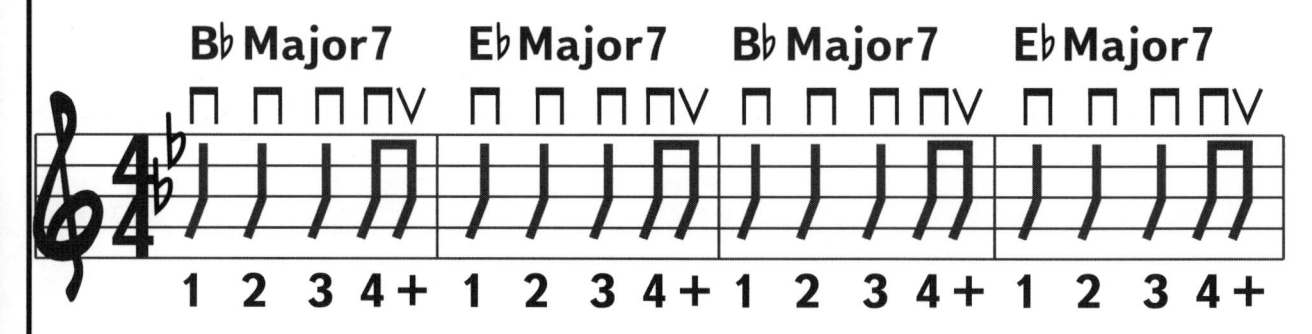

FIG.153 - MINI-SONG USING MAJOR 7TH CHORDS

70 UKULELE BEGINNERS JUMPSTART: A SEEING MUSIC METHOD BOOK

DAY 12 - PLAY YOUR FIRST SONGS

MILESTONE

Just think of all the chords you've learned in just a few days.

Remember all the combinations of rhythms and time signatures you've used.

Time give yourself a pat on the back for assembling all this knowledge in a short amount of time!

HOW TO PLAY JINGLE BELLS

These are classic songs that will demonstrate the many chords and rhythms you've learned.

Play these first 4 bars of Jingle Bells with all downstrokes, 3 per measure. This is a good way to learn any song, starting with a simple rhythm. Does this section look pretty easy? Yes, it is!

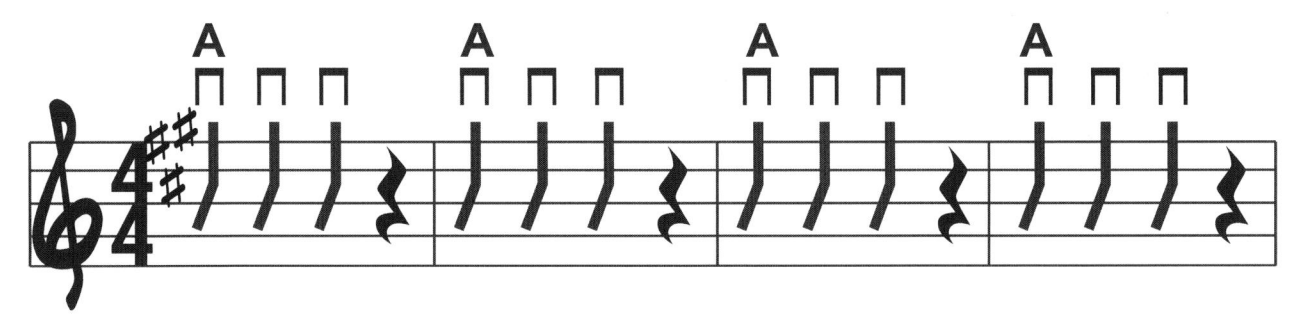

FIG.154 - "JINGLE BELLS" OPENING MEASURES

On the next page you'll see the full song with a much more interesting rhythm. As you're getting familiar with the chord changes, feel free to substitute the more simple, all downstroke rhythm until you get comfortable.

Jingle Bells

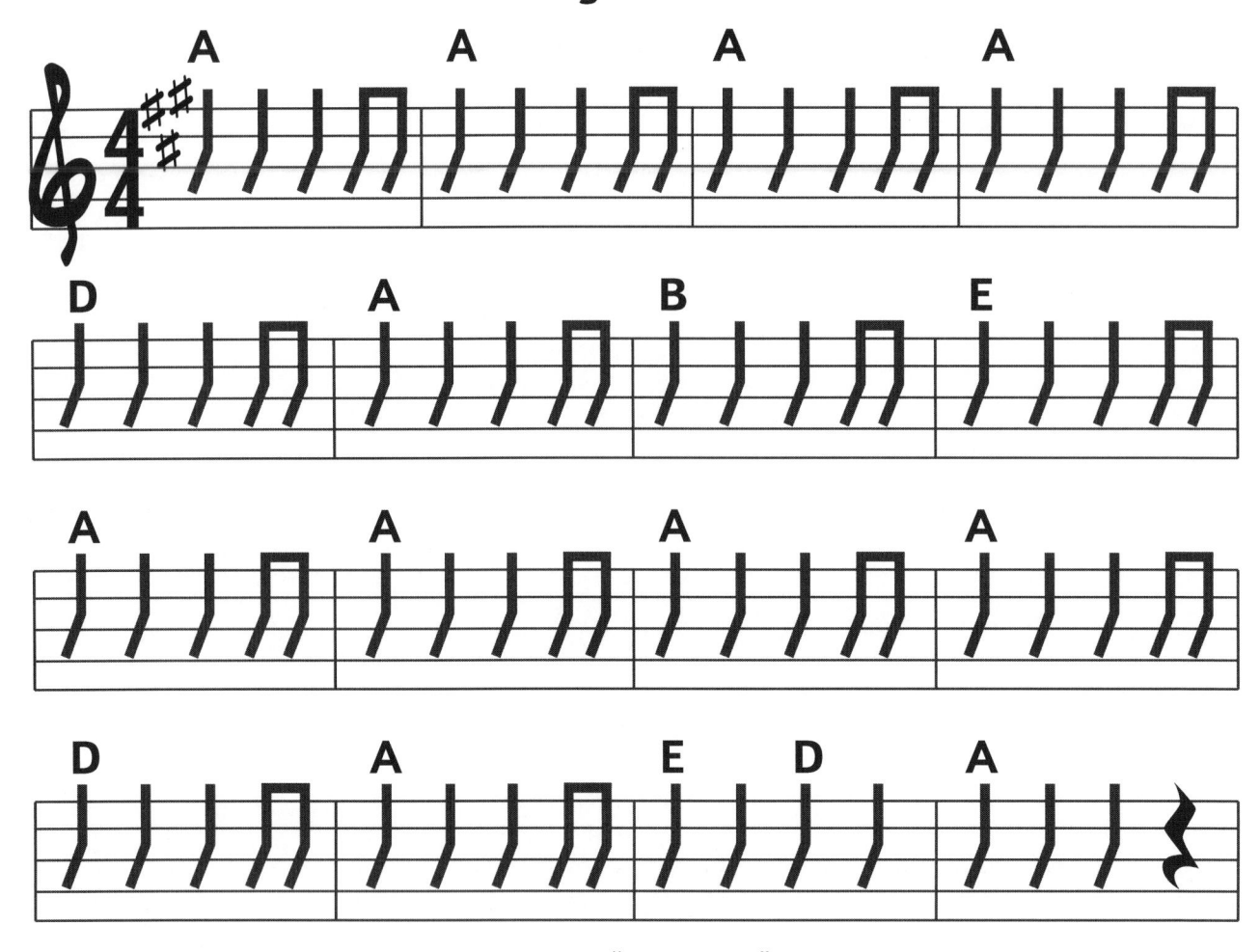

FIG.155 - "JINGLE BELLS"

HOW TO PLAY HAPPY BIRTHDAY

Here's a song everyone loves to hear! Again, feel free to start with all downstrokes until the chord changes are smooth and connected.

Happy Birthday

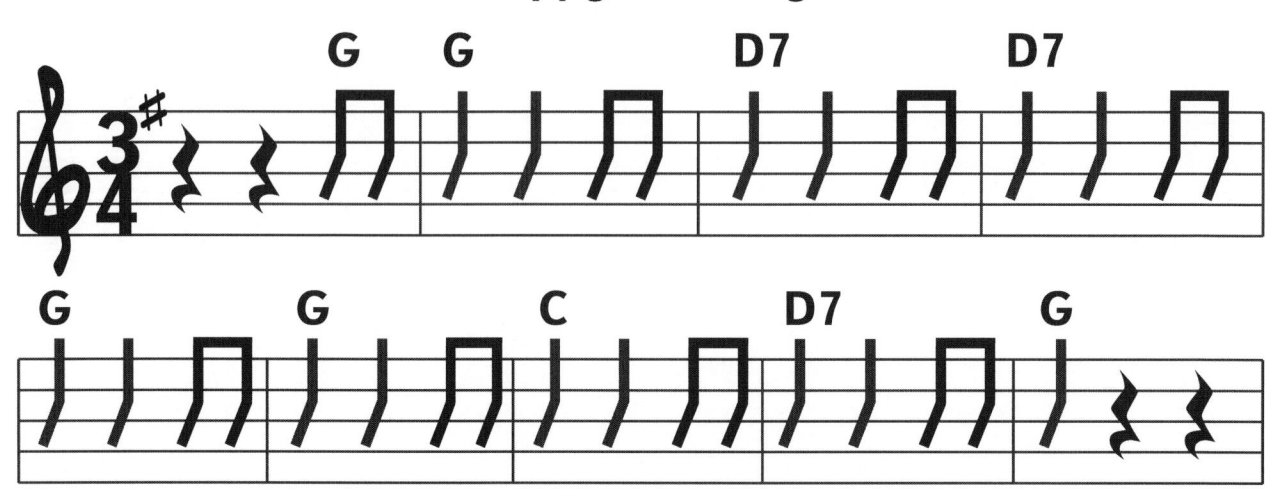

FIG.156 - "HAPPY BIRTHDAY"

72 UKULELE BEGINNERS JUMPSTART: A SEEING MUSIC METHOD BOOK

HOW TO PLAY A BLUES SONG

Blues music is recognized and enjoyed everywhere in the world. Perhaps one of the reasons it is so popular is because it has so many varieties.

Additionally, Blues music evolved into Rock and Roll, Country music and much of Jazz. It's certainly a form worth studying!

There are two chords here you haven't seen before, still they should look vaguely familiar.

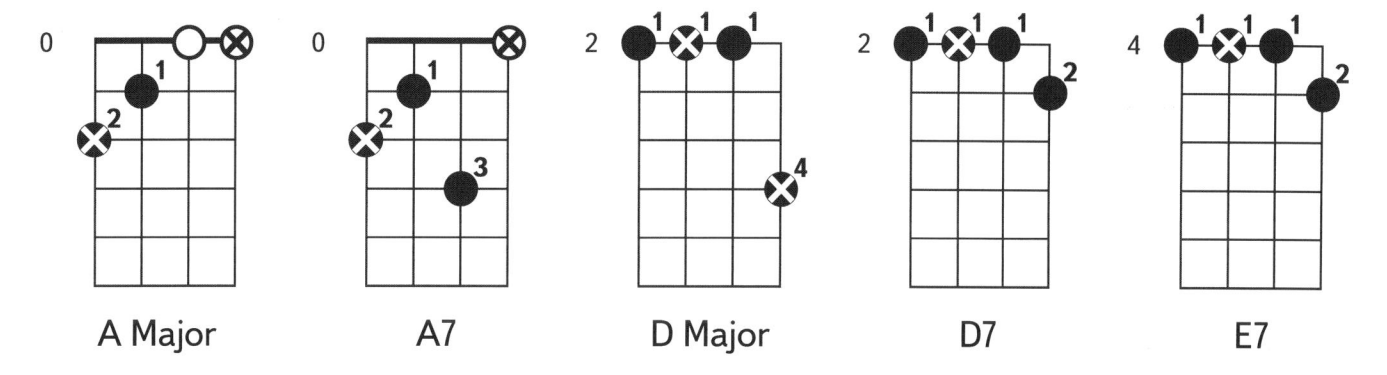

A Major   A7   D Major   D7   E7

A Major Blues

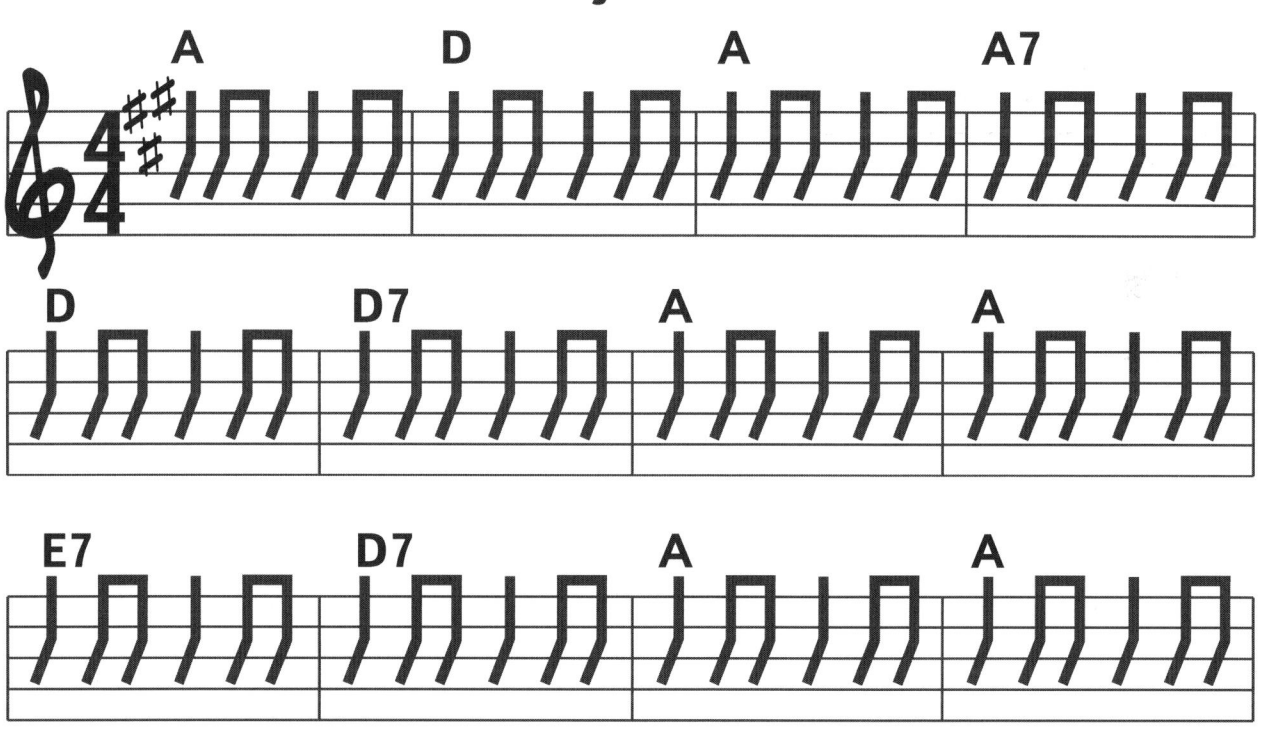

FIG.157 - A MAJOR BLUES

HOW TO PLAY A ROCK AND ROLL SONG

Early Rock and Roll took the familiar chord changes of the Blues and started mixing things up. Often the two forms would use the same chords, but Rock and Roll would recombine them, putting a new twist on familiar chords. See how much this song sounds like the Blues.

PLAY YOUR FIRST SONGS 73

F Major Rock and Roll

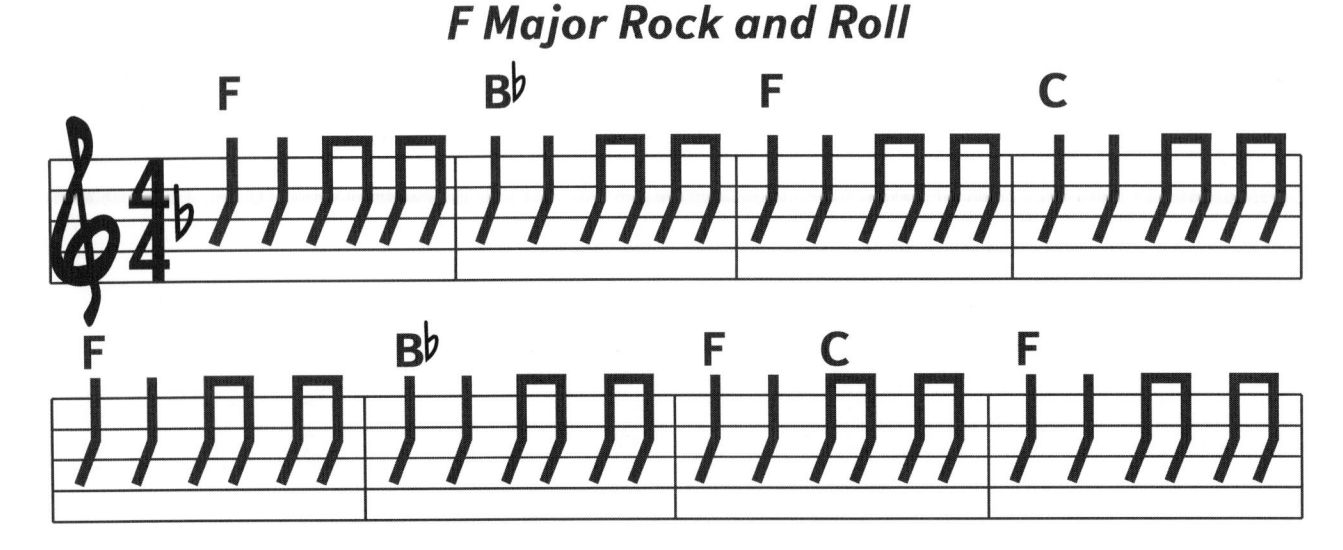

FIG.158 - F MAJOR ROCK AND ROLL

ROCK AND ROLL WITH MINOR CHORDS

Early Rock and Roll music certainly wasn't afraid to experiment! Here's an example of 1950s-style rock using major and minor chords.

This song uses an eighth-note rest followed by an eighth-note, like this:

Play a reststroke on the eighth-rest followed by an upstroke on the next eighth-note.

C Major Rock and Roll

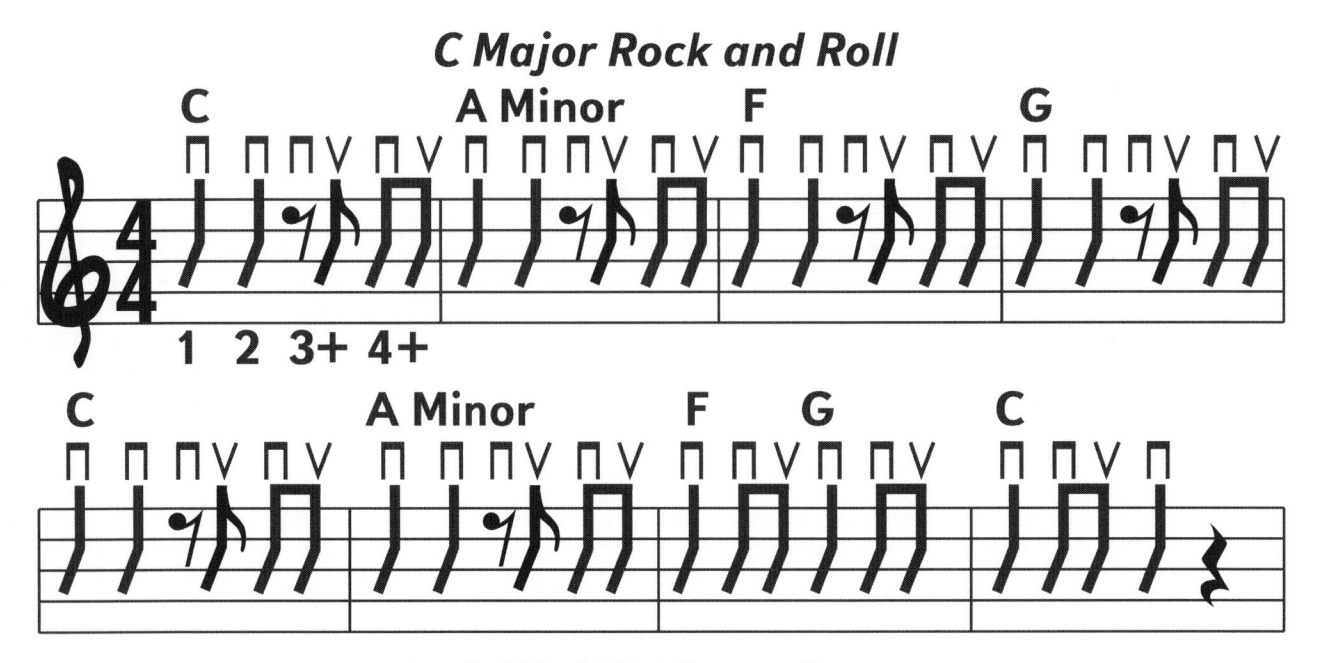

1 2 3+ 4+

FIG.159 - C MAJOR ROCK AND ROLL

74 UKULELE BEGINNERS JUMPSTART: A SEEING MUSIC METHOD BOOK

ASSIGNMENT

Today's Assignment

Continue practicing the songs in this chapter. Then, try making up your own songs with combinations of chords and rhythms you like. Are you ready? Of course you are!

Of course, you may not like every combination of chords you try. That's normal. Write down the chord combinations and rhythms you find interesting on the sheet music below.

PLAY YOUR FIRST SONGS 75

UKULELE BEGINNERS JUMPSTART

MILESTONES IN MUSIC

Time to congratulate yourself on all you've learned!

- How to read fretboard diagrams
- Note names through the first 5 frets
- Time signatures and note values (eighth, quarter, half)
- Major and minor chords
- Many commonly used strumming rhythms
- C Major and D Major scales
- Three varieties of 7th chords
- Traditional, Blues and Rock and Roll Songs

Today's Assignment

Keep learning! You're well on your way to total ukulele and musical knowledge! Explore the vast world of music and dive into everything you find interesting. You already have to tools to make music and begin answering the questions you'll discover along the way.

There are several books in the Seeing Music family you may find interesting to develop your knowledge and skill. Seeing Music books put you inside the mind of professional string players everywhere who organize their vast knowledge by very simple visual means. Our books give you the tools to continue teaching yourself, to be able to play anything, anytime.

Keep on makin' music, musician!

Spell Major and Minor Scales
Create Major, Minor and Diminished Chords
Master the 7 Modes of Major Scales
Basic Improvisation and Soloing Strategies
Create 7th, 9th and Suspended Chords
SEEING MUSIC
METHOD BOOKS
Music Theory Explained in Practical, Everyday Context for All Genres
LEFT-HANDED
GUITAR THEORY
NUTS & BOLTS
ANDY SCHNEIDER
BEGINNER TO INTERMEDIATE
LEFT-HANDED GUITAR
BEGINNERS
JUMPSTART
BEGINNER
BEGINNER TO INTERMEDIATE
ANDY SCHNEIDER
Just for Lefties! We've got your books, too.
SeeingMusicBooks.com
SEEING MUSIC
METHOD BOOKS

CHORD AND NOTE REFERENCE

Note Names

Similar Fingerings

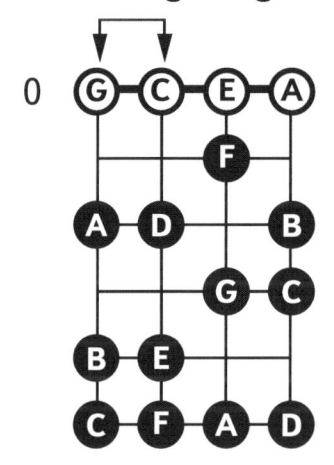

FIG.160 - NATURAL NOTES

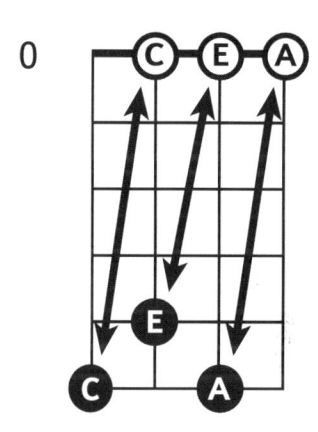

FIG.161 - NOTE NAME EQUIVALENTS

Major Chords

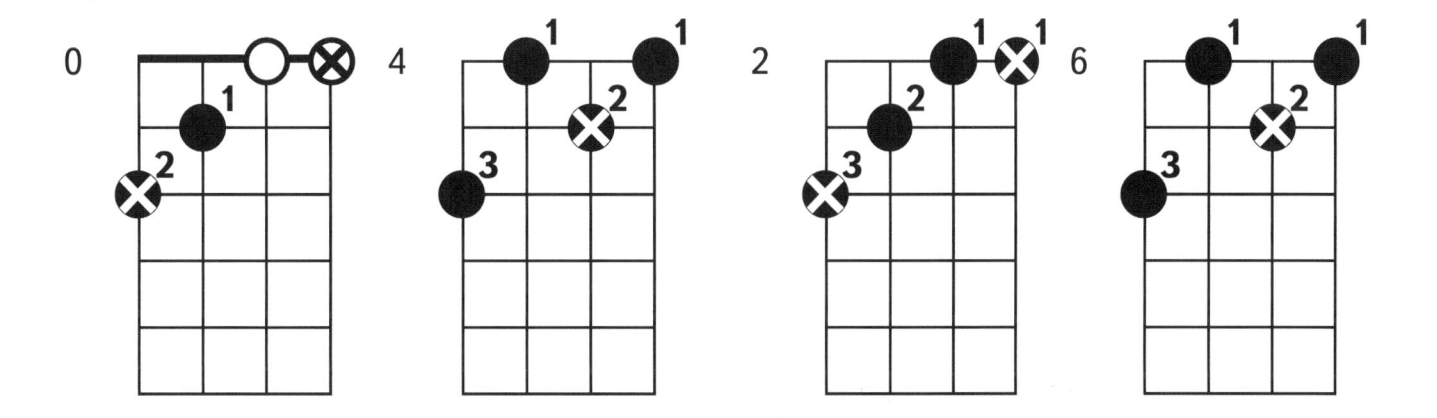

FIG.162 - A MAJOR

FIG.163 - B MAJOR

Major Chords (cont.)

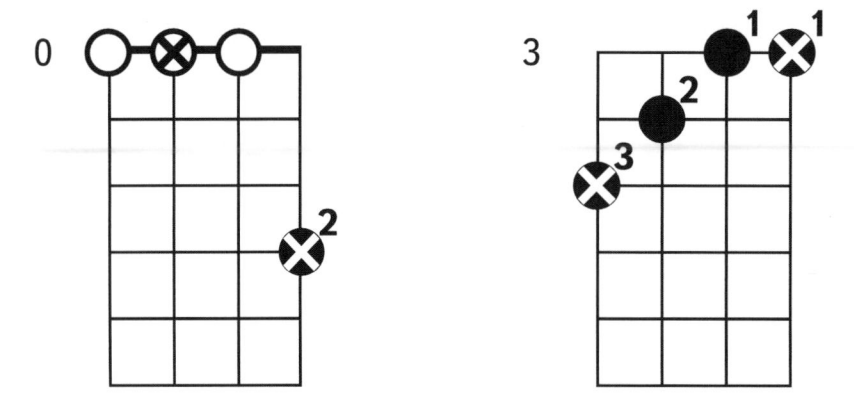

Fig.164 - C Major

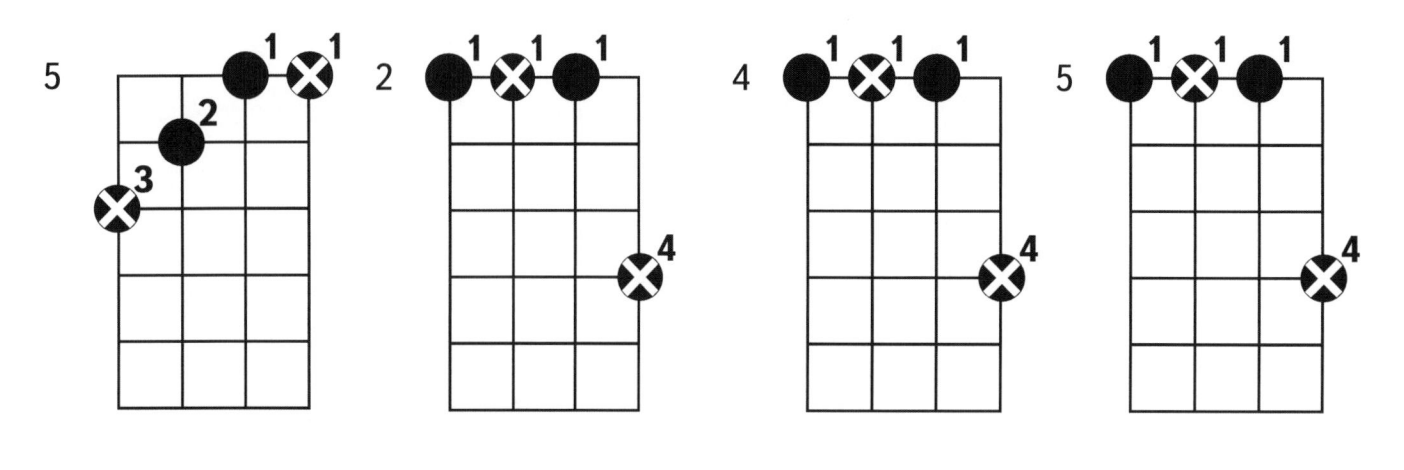

Fig.165 - D Major

Fig.166 - E Major

Fig.167 - F Major

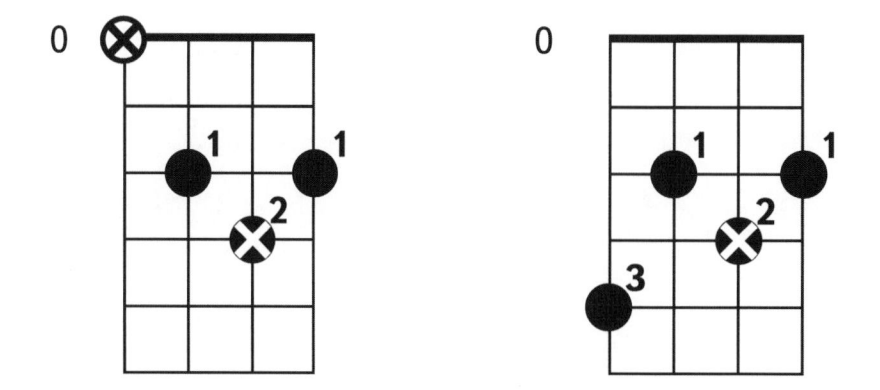

Fig.168 - G Major

80 UKULELE BEGINNERS JUMPSTART: A SEEING MUSIC METHOD BOOK

Minor Chords

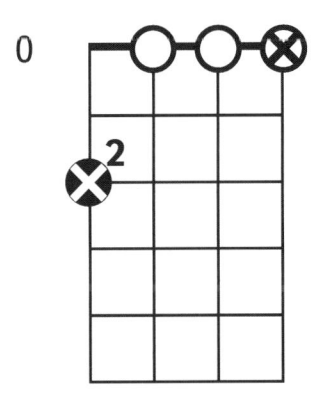

Fig.169 - A Minor

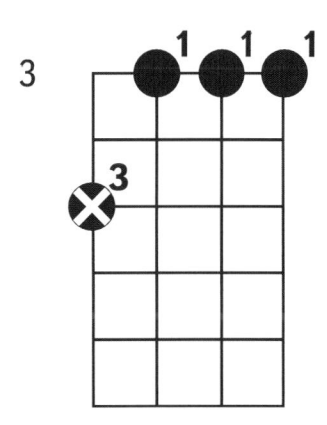

Fig.170 - C Minor

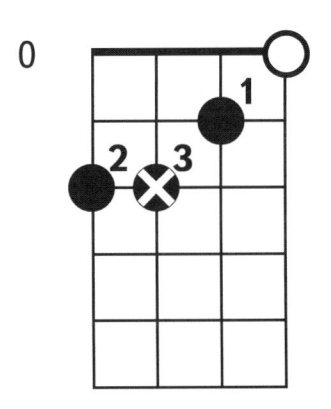

Fig.171 - D Minor

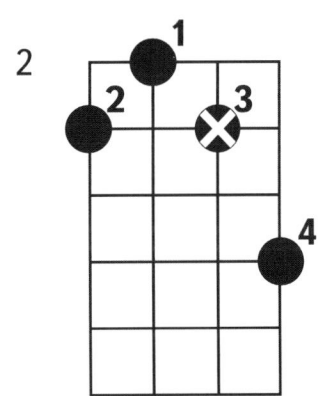

Fig.172 - G Minor

CHORD AND NOTE REFERENCE 81

Extended Chords

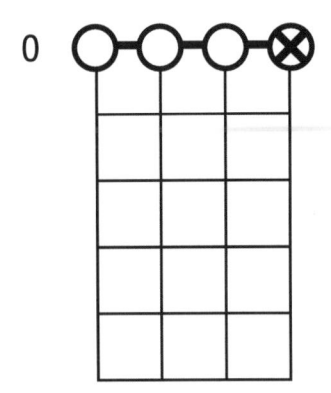

Fig.173 - A minor7

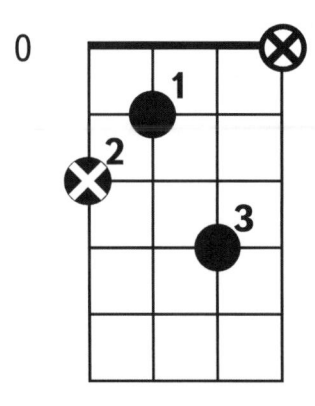

Fig.174 - A7

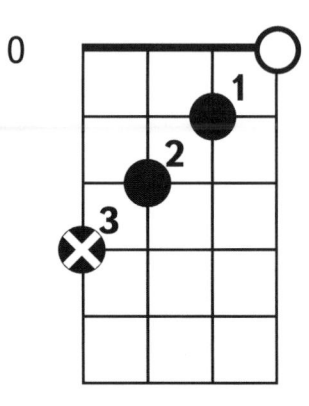

Fig.175 - B flat Major 7

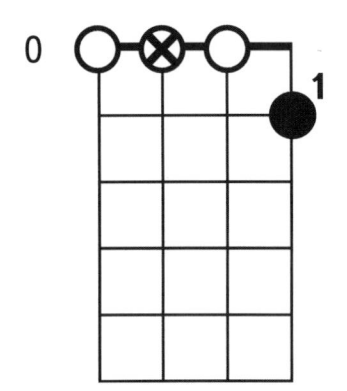

Fig.176 - C7

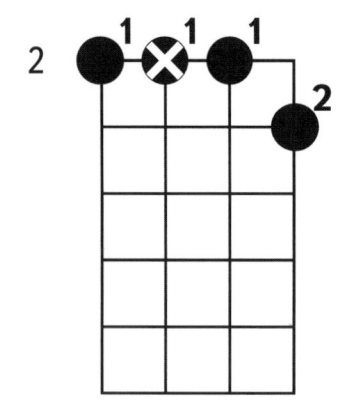

Fig.177 - D7

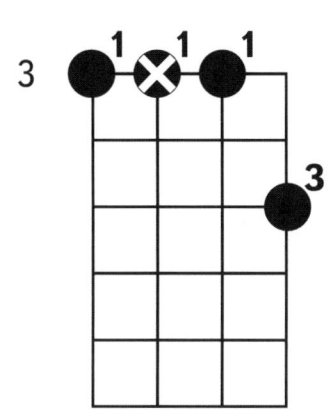

Fig.178 - E flat Major 7

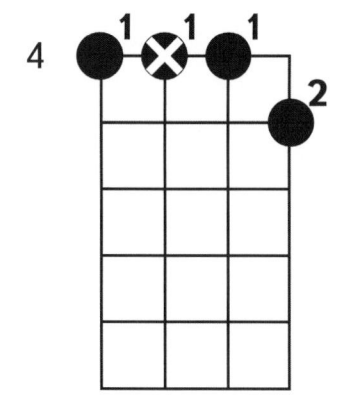

Fig.179 - E7

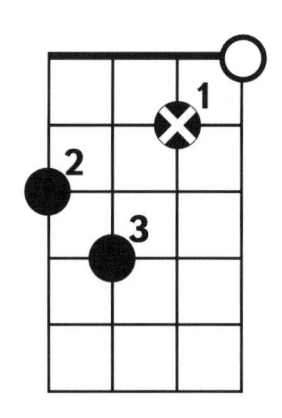

Fig.180 - F7

82 UKULELE BEGINNERS JUMPSTART: A SEEING MUSIC METHOD BOOK

Scales

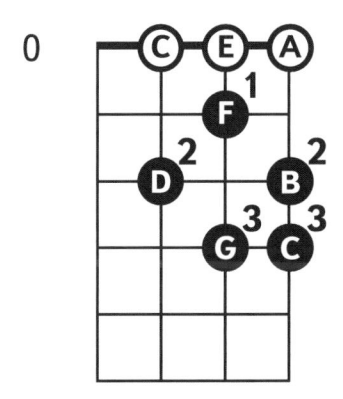

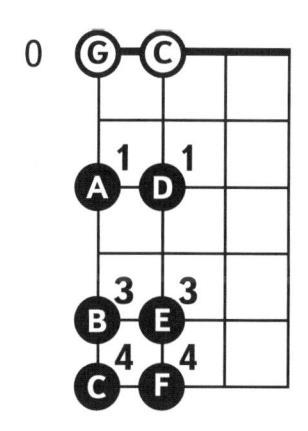

FIG. 181 - C Major Scales

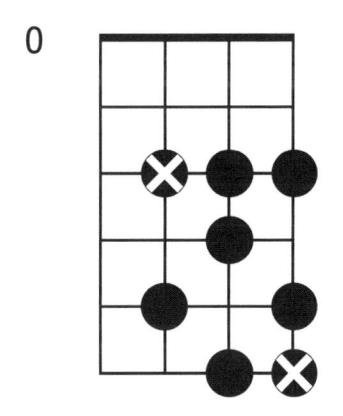

FIG. 182 - D Major Scale

Blank Fretboard Diagrams

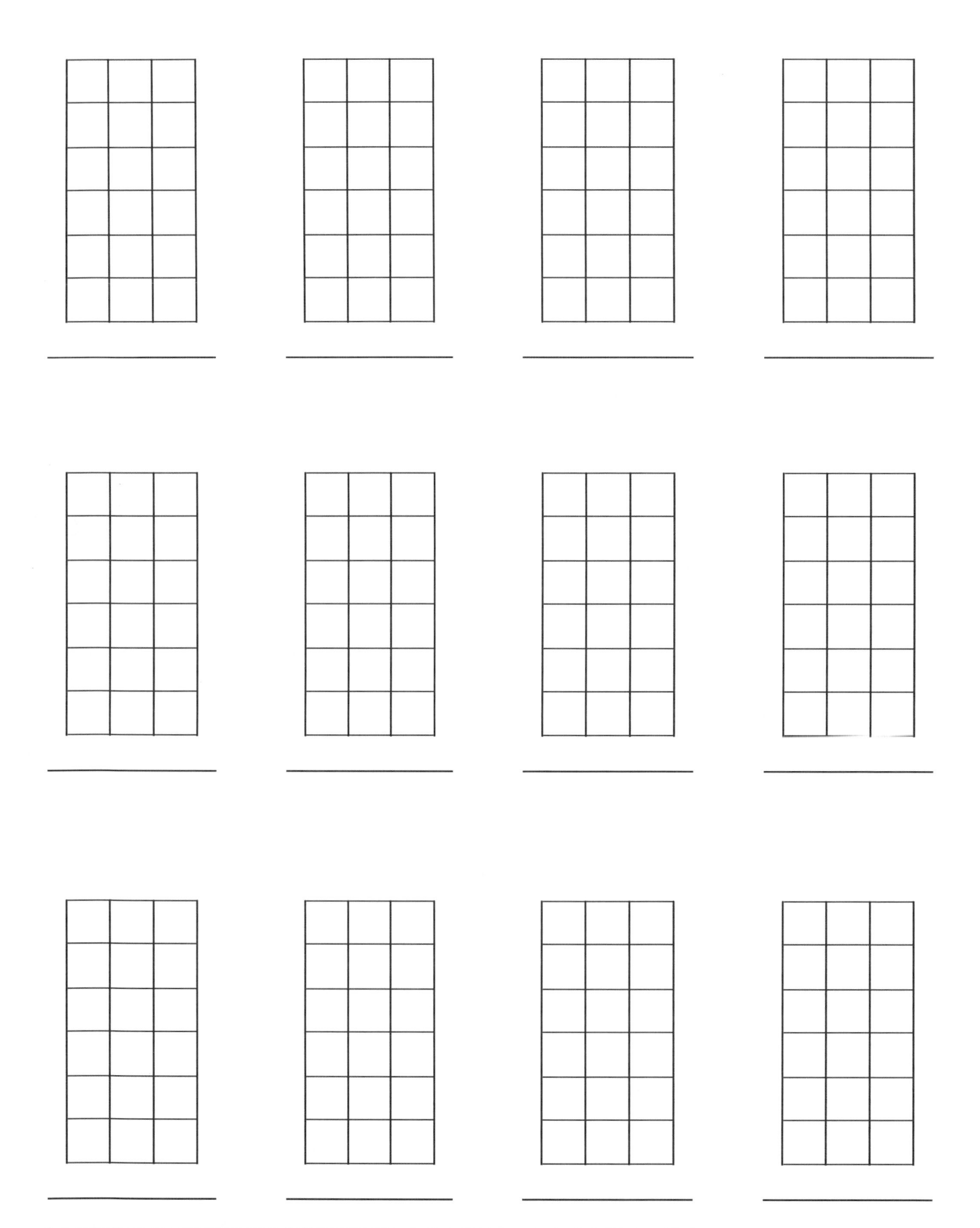

84 UKULELE BEGINNERS JUMPSTART: A SEEING MUSIC METHOD BOOK

Printed in Great Britain
by Amazon